The
Golden
Formula

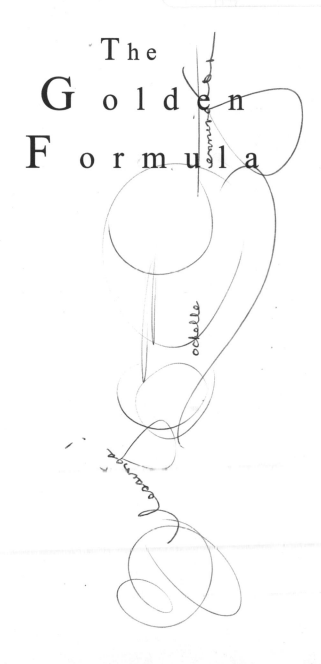

The
Golden
Formula

Use Divine Principles to Harvest
More Happiness, Prosperity, and
Joy in Your Life

Rochelle Pennington

ISBN: 0-9740810-0-0

Dedicated with gratitude
to my Dad and Mom
who knew the value of living lovingly

Table of Contents

Chapter 1 – The Multiplication Table of God

Table of Contents

Chapter 2 – Living Lovingly

Table of Contents

Chapter 3 – Turning From Anger to Forgiveness

9

Table of Contents

Chapter 4 – Choosing an Attitude

Table of Contents

Chapter 5 – I Believe!

Introduction

A long time has passed since I attended Sunday School classes in the backroom of the little white chapel in my hometown.

It was there that, as a youngster, I learned all about the Bible verse that had its own nickname: "The Golden Rule."

I liked this nickname. Particularly, I liked the word "golden." This one word made me pay attention a bit better. Although just a little girl, I knew that "golden" stuff meant good stuff.

The kids in our neighborhood agreed on this, and so we spent many an afternoon on our bicycles chasing after rainbows in search of the pot of gold that was to be found at their end. Down our village streets we raced, around corners, and through open fields, really fast. But the end of the rainbow – and the gold – eluded us always.

It was not until I grew older that I began to understand that we had been looking for treasures in the wrong places. I began to realize that the real treasure hunt begins within.

Written on a chalkboard back at the old chapel were the words: "Do to others as you would have them do to you, The Golden Rule." These words were required memorization for all of us. This teaching was emphasized, plain and simple. Now I know why. It's because it is a good teaching, as good as gold.

In the pages that follow you will discover how this "golden rule" underlies all of life and is an equation, a formula, a type of mathematical measurer of cause and effect. In the true stories and observations shared, you will become aware of the importance of this single sentence and learn how to apply its wisdom to your own life in order to fill it with the blessings of love, joy, and peace. And what, I ask, is worth more than these?

You will discover how this spiritual formula has the power to transform every area of your life and learn that by beginning from the inner places within your own heart, you can – and will - change your outer world.

Can a single sentence really hold such promise? Quite simply, yes. And each of us has equal access to the choices that set its power in motion for our good.

The Golden Rule. It is a behavioral guideline for humankind with curious words reminding us to reflect on what it is we wish others to do to us before we do to them.

Whether you've heard these words a hundred times, a thousand times, or more times than you can remember, consider them again in the voices that speak in the pages that follow. Then see if you will not agree that they truly are a treasure and your rainbow is within.

Stand at the crossroads and look;
ask for the ancient paths,
ask where the good way is and walk in it,
and you will find rest for your souls.
Jeremiah 6:16

CHAPTER 1

The Multiplication Table of God

Harvesting a Bumper Crop of Blessings

It is a great day in a man's experience when he makes up his mind that within himself, under his control, are the forces that can make his life victorious.

Harry Emerson Fosdick

My grandparents were farmers. They lived in a big, old house on a little plot of land in rural Wisconsin, eighty acres total. In this house hung a painting. You couldn't help but notice it. It was really quite remarkable.

On the canvas was painted a field of ripened corn - acres and acres and acres of corn. An old man in bib overalls was walking into it. With him was a little girl, and these two were carrying baskets. Bushel baskets, to be exact.

The painting is long gone, as are my grandparents, but what I learned in the house it hung in is not. And it is this: There is a law that governs the promise of harvest, a law that applies to all of life - to fields and to our fellows. Simply put, the law is this: that which is sown will be that which is grown.

Grandpapa said it this way, "You can't plant tomatoes and expect to harvest beans."

It's a simple truth. And it was this truth that my grandfather used to harvest his land and to harvest his heart. With each, his land and his life, the same principle was at work, the exact same. He knew this. The reality of what he experienced in love and in joy and in peace was the direct result of what he purposed for. And so it is with us.

Do we desire more love in our lives? More kindness? More friendship? Then we must seed our lives with loving acts and with kindly deeds. Then, the harvest comes. Again, that which is sown will be that which is grown. Beans from beans. Corn from corn. Love from love. There's no other way.

Is it really that easy? Does it really work? Can it work in your life? The answer is yes. And yes and yes. So get your basket ready.

Seed by seed, deed by deed, we turn the soil of our souls over in our lives and plant something there, and that something begins to grow - unseen at the first, but not at the last. Be sure of it.

Just for today, try this. Try beginning your morning by speaking the following affirmation: "I purpose in my heart to seek love in the coming day. In seeking love, and in being loving, I will harvest more love in my life. For that which is sown will be that which is grown. My harvest is coming and my basket is ready."

Try the affirmation for today. Then try it again tomorrow, and the day after that. Then fill those days with loving moments - with hellos and handshakes and hugs. Smile at folks. Wave. Pick up the phone and call an old friend to ask, "So, how have you been?"

Harvesting a loving life is not about participating in the momentous, but rather, about participating - daily and consistently - in little, loving moments. Just moments.

Like holding the door open for the person walking into the grocery store behind you, or wishing another person a good day - with sincerity, or shoveling the snow off a neighbor's walkway, or visiting a nursing home where someone who loves you very much is waiting for you to come by.

We love one another in moments - in the moments it takes to sing a lullaby or to read a story or to catch a little fellow at the end of a slide. We love one another in the time it takes to fix a family member's favorite supper or to bake a batch of cookies to share at the office. We love one another in the time it takes to get up early to put the coffee on or to slip a love note into a lunch box.

It's the moments that matter most. Little moments spent seeking love and being love. Then, the seeds from these deeds start growing. When we shift our focus off of what we expect from others and place it, instead, on to what we can give of ourselves, everything in life changes. Absolutely everything. Know this: The blessings we experience in our own lives will be in direct proportion to the blessings we have brought into the lives of others.

So, begin today. Begin with the affirmation. This will establish purpose. But remember, first and foremost, that it is our actual participation in loving deeds that will seed our harvest.

As an example, I ask you this: If my grandpa only *planned* a crop of corn, would he have had a harvest? If he only *said*, "I sure do want some corn to grow in that field yonder" would the corn have grown? Nope, sure wouldn't have. With the planning, there must be planting. Lands or lives, the same holds true.

Bountiful blessings are within our reach, blessings beyond measure - acres and acres and acres of them. Every time we choose to love, we take one step closer to our harvest, a harvest that begins to grow beneath the dawn of each new day, including this one.

So let's get our baskets ready and meet one another there.

The Multiplication Table of God

We receive but what we give.

Samuel Coleridge

$1 - 1 = 1$ (God does His math a little differently than we do.)

In this equation's simplest explanation, the Divine Formula of $1 - 1 = 1$ goes like this: whatever we give away is returned back to us. And since all religions touch on this concept of "sowing and reaping" in some way or another, it has come to be known as The Universal Law.

God's "fixed laws of heaven and earth (Jeremiah 33:25 NIV)" are woven into the fabric of His creation; they do not work for one person and not for another. The law of sowing and reaping is not unlike the law of gravity. The law of gravity - a fixed law of earth - works the same for everyone, regardless of faith belief, just as the law of sowing and reaping does.

The understandings between faith communities regarding the law of sowing and reaping vary only in the final sum. Several beliefs maintain that what we give away (or send out from our being) is returned to us evenly, while many tend to hold to the belief that what we give away is multiplied – at least by 2 or as much as 100! – before being returned to us.

Drawing an example from Christian Scripture we read:

"Be not deceived; God is not mocked: for whatsoever a man soweth, that shall he also reap (Galatians 6:7 KJV)."

If we bless others, God will bless us. We like this idea, especially when taking into consideration the possibility of a multiplication. *God is really good*!

A word of warning, though, to look more closely. "Whatsoever" not only encompasses love, kindness, generosity, gratitude, joy, peace, and forgiveness, but also hate, anger, fear, worry, gossip, criticism and negativity (with the possibility, once again, of a multiplication.) PANIC! *How could God do that to us*!? If this thought makes us uncomfortable, it's meant to.

Sooner or later we will come to the realization that our own personal behavior and attitude toward our fellow human beings has more to do with the quality of our life than we probably care to admit.

If our life lacks light, we must honestly (and perhaps painfully) reflect on what it is we are sending out from our being for, ultimately, it is not God who withholds goodness and blessing from us, we withhold them from ourselves.

$1 - 1 = 1$ Study this equation carefully. You will be tested every day.

The game of life is the game of boomerangs. Our thoughts, words, and deeds return to us – sooner or later – with astounding accuracy.

Florence Shinn

We Cannot Give Without Receiving

What we do today, right now, will have an accumulated effect on all of our tomorrows.

Alexandra Stoddard

"The wise man," said Lao-tzu, "does not lay up treasure. The more he gives to others, the more he has for his own."

Have you ever seen a truly generous person who was not genuinely happy? Have you ever seen a miser who was not basically miserable?

Have you ever seen a generous person who really lacked for anything? Perhaps he did not have every luxury, but in all probability he was content, joyous, abundantly rich in friends.

Let me share with you one of the most joyous hobbies any human being can ever engage in. My hobby is giving something away every day - something tangible, so that I will be reminded to give away the vastly more important intangibles: a smile, a word of encouragement, an intercessory prayer, a telephone call or a letter to some lonely person.

Every day I give something away. It may be a book, a poster, a flower, a poem, a plaque with an inspirational message - something that will enrich the life of the recipient.

For this I know: The more I give to others, the more I have.

Among the rich rewards are friends who love me. I experience the daily satisfaction that I have made life happier for at least one person. I have an inner peace that comes from the assurance that truly it is better to give than to receive. The truth is, we cannot give without receiving...in abundance...to overflowing.

William Arthur Ward

What are the Odds?

The heart that gives, gathers.

Hannah Moore

Twenty years ago, a car accident claimed the life of longtime Augusta National Golf Club Manager Phil Wahl. Janice, his widow, was left with nine children. Phil's friends wanted to help.

As the club's photographer, I had gotten to know Phil pretty well. The idea of a golf tournament to raise funds for his family seemed like a good one, so I made a few phone calls and was heartened by the overwhelming response.

The benefit tournament was set for West Lake, a popular Augusta country club that donated use of its course. Fee was set at one thousand dollars per player. The first obstacle was that some of Phil's friends could not afford the fee; still they wanted to show their support. While agonizing over this dilemma, I received a phone call from a member of the National who wished to remain anonymous. He offered to put up the fee for those who could not afford it. We were off and running!

Fifty-five players came out, including such notables as Jack Nicklaus, Ken Venturi, David Graham, Chris Schenkel and Ed Sneed. One of the first guys to sign up was Slicker Sam of Chicago, an internationally known golfer who regularly played for large sums of money - and usually won.

Anyone who knew Slicker agreed he should be deemed a national treasure. I say this because of his reputation for charity.

At the end of play, we gathered in the dining room for tournament awards. A substantial prize - a luxurious new Cadillac donated by a local dealer - stood out from the usual closest-to-pin and longest drive awards. All eyes were riveted on the shiny new set of keys that Master of Ceremonies Ken Venturi held up. After a long, dramatic pause, Ken finally smiled, and said: "Come on up, Slicker Sam, and claim your prize!"

Silence fell over the room as Slicker Sam moved to the podium. He was quite a champion. Ken handed him the keys.

Slicker Sam had broken 70 to claim the victory, but only at that moment were we to learn why he had played with so much determination.

"I already have a car!" Sam said to Venturi, returning the keys. "Please, give this Cadillac to Phil Wahl's family!"

The room responded with a standing ovation. That was class, Slicker-style.

The following day, Slicker and Doug Sanders had arranged to play for some serious money. Doug's playing partner was singer Andy Williams. I was the fourth. We played the match in Aiken, South Carolina, about fourteen miles east of Augusta, at the Houndslake Golf Club.

As we rode down the first fairway I remembered I had been given some raffle tickets to sell on behalf of a synagogue in Augusta. Each ticket cost a hundred dollars and was good for a chance at the grand prize. Doug, Andy and Slicker all purchased tickets.

A few weeks later I attended a dinner where the raffle tickets were pulled, eliminating contenders. As the night wore on, all names were eliminated except two, and Slicker Sam remained in the race. When someone else's name was called, my heart dropped. I thought they were declaring a winner. I was wrong. Slicker Sam was the winner!

His prize? A brand new Cadillac! What are the odds of that?

I guess some things are ordained by a higher power. There's one thing I know for sure: Sam had been rewarded for his wonderful generosity.

Frank Christian

Life's Mirror

There are loyal hearts, there are spirits brave,
There are souls that are pure and true;
Then give to the world the best you have
And the best will come back to you.

Give love, and love to your heart will flow,
A strength in your utmost need;
Have faith, and a score of hearts will show
Their faith in your word and deed.

Give truth, and your gift will be paid in kind,
And honor will honor meet;
And a smile that is sweet will surely find
A smile that is just as sweet.

For life is the mirror of king and slave -
Tis what you are and do;
Then give to the world the best you have
And the best will come back to you.

Madeline Bridges

Giving never moves in a straight line — it always travels in circles.

Robert Schuller

Things Turned Rosy

The merciful man doeth good to his own soul.
Proverbs 11:17 KJV

Smoke poured out from under the front hood of the black stretch limousine as it sped down the highway. Louis, the limousine's chauffeur, pulled over on the roadside to flag down assistance. Concern and worry were written on his face. He stood in the cold rain and frantically waved a flashlight in the air, hoping to draw people to his plight. It was futile. Most drivers slowed down to catch a glimpse of the stalled limousine, but then continued on their way.

Robert Wise was the exception. He noted the chauffeur's predicament and felt compelled to come to his aid. He drove up to the shoulder of the road, peered out his window, and asked how he could help.

"Would you please call my boss and tell him my situation?" asked the chauffeur. "And then could you please come back here and let me know what he says?"

"No problem," came the cheerful reply. Louis then provided Robert with the name of his boss, Mr. Cavendish, and a phone number. Robert got back on the highway, drove to the nearest service station, and made the call.

A short time later, Robert returned. He relayed a message from Mr. Cavendish and then turned on his engine, ready to continue on his way home.

"Wait!" Louis called out to him. "How can I thank you?"

"Oh, please, it was nothing," replied Robert.

"No, you must tell me how I can thank you," the chauffeur insisted.

"It was really nothing," came the reply, "but if you care to, you can send a dozen roses to my wife for her birthday, which is next week." Robert gave Louis his address, and the two men departed.

The following day, the chauffeur told his boss what had happened on the road. He described how difficult it had been to get assistance and how glad he had been when a kind stranger finally stopped to help. "And all the man asked for were flowers for his wife," concluded the chauffeur.

Mr. Cavendish listened and was touched by Robert's modest request. He took the address and said, "Leave the rest to me."

Within the next few days, Mr. Cavendish arranged for flowers to be sent to Robert Wise's home. But that was not all. For years, the couple had been struggling financially and were threatened with foreclosure. They were now blessed with a generosity of spirit, for in addition to the dozen red roses, Mr. Cavendish graciously paid off the mortgage on their house.

> Yitta Halberstam
> and Judith Leventhal

To Give or Not to Give

Assume responsibility for the quality of your life.
Norman Cousins

The Sea of Galilee and the Dead Sea are made of the same water. It flows down, clear and cool, from Mount Hermon and from the roots of the cedars of Lebanon.

The Sea of Galilee makes beauty of it, for the Sea of Galilee has an outlet. *It gives.* It gathers in its riches and then pours them out again to fertilize the Jordan plain.

But the Dead Sea, with the same water, makes horror. For the Dead Sea has no outlet. *It keeps.*

That is the radical difference between selfish and unselfish people.

We all want life's enriching blessings. We ought to; they are Divine gifts. But some of us then *give*, and are like the Sea of Galilee; while others *keep*, and they are like the brackish waters that cover the Dead Sea.

Harry Emerson Fosdick

A Change of Heart

The root word of "miserable" is miser.
Cullen Hightower

"*Oh! But he was a tight-fisted hand at the grindstone; a squeezing, wrenching, grasping, scraping, clutching, covetous old sinner! Hard and sharp as flint; self-contained, and solitary as an oyster. The cold within him froze his old features, nipped his pointed nose, shriveled his cheeks, made his thin lips blue. He carried his own low temperature always about with him. External heat and cold had little influence on him. No warmth could warm, nor wintry weather chill him. No wind that blew was bitterer than he.*"

Thus begins Charles Dicken's narrative description of Scrooge, a beast of a fellow so disagreeable that a young caroler flees from him "in terror," two gentlemen attempting to collect a donation to help the poor are given nothing, and a nephew's invitation to join his family for Christmas dinner, flatly rejected.

Such is Scrooge....to begin with. But then, only one night (and four ghosts) later, the description takes a curious turn:

"*'I am as light as a feather, I am as happy as an angel, I am as merry as a schoolboy!' cried Scrooge. 'A merry Christmas to everybody! A happy New Year to all the world!'*

"He went to church, and walked about the streets, and watched the people hurrying to and fro, and patted children on the head, and questioned beggars, and looked down into the kitchens of houses, and up to the windows, and found that everything could yield him pleasure. He never dreamed that any walk - that anything - could give him so much happiness! And to Tiny Tim, who did not die, he was a second father. He became as good a friend, as good a master, and as good a man as the good old city knew, or any other good old city, town, or borough in the good old world. Some people laughed to see the alteration in him, but he let them laugh, and little heeded them, for he was wise enough to know that nothing ever happened on this globe, for good, at which some people did not have their fill of laughter in the outset. His own heart laughed, and that was quite enough for him."

Same man, same story. What happened?

I believe the answer lies in Dicken's carefully chosen words "self-contained, and solitary as an oyster." These details described not only the man, but the reason for his misery. Scrooge would come to learn that happiness is the result of directing the light within one's heart - kindness, generosity, love, joy - toward others.

Not to direct our light outward is to extinguish it - *even unto ourselves.*

There is a destiny that makes us brothers; none goes his way alone. All that we send into the lives of others, comes back into our own.

Edwin Markham

Choosing the Way of Your Soul

To every man there openeth a way,
and ways, and a way.

And the high soul climbs the high way,
and the low soul gropes the low,
and in between, on the misty flats,
the rest drift to and fro.

But to every man there openeth
a high way, and a low.
And every man decideth
the way his soul shall go.

William Dunkerley

Arthur Berry's Answer

It's a sad day when you find out that it's not accident
or time or fortune, but just yourself, that kept things from you.
Lillian Hellman

Arthur Berry was a very famous jewel thief who prac-
ticed his trade back in the roaring 20's. He was a very
unusual thief in that he would only steal from the very rich.
Not only did they have to be rich, but they had to be of the
elite rich. The story goes that Arthur would pass up many
jewels and take only the finest, most precious. He was one
thief that was a connoisseur of art. Since Arthur Berry stole
only from the highest elite of society it became something of
a social status to have been robbed by this notorious robber.
This kind of widespread popularity gave the police night-
mares.

Well, one day Arthur stole one too many times because
the police caught him in the act, and he was shot. While he
was suffering excruciating pain he promised himself that he
would never steal again. Now, that was a good beginning,
but, for some strange happening, Arthur escaped his impris-
onment and spent three more years on the loose. Then came
his downfall, when an insanely jealous woman turned on
him by telling the police where he was. He was recaptured
and spent the next eighteen years behind bars.

While in prison, Arthur made up his mind that crime didn't pay and that he would never steal again.

When Arthur got out of prison he made his way to a little town up in New England and settled down. People did not suspect that he was a famous jewel thief, and due to his hard work and neighborliness, he soon became one of the small town's respected citizens.

All went well with Arthur until someone came to the little town and recognized him as the famous jewel thief. As the news spread as to who he was, reporters came rushing in from the largest city newspapers to interview this reformed criminal. One of the questions that was put to Arthur by a young reporter was this one: "Arthur, we know that you have taken from some of the wealthiest people in the world. Do you remember who it was that you stole the most from?" Without a moment's hesitation Arthur answered, "The person that I stole the most from was Arthur Berry. I could have made a contribution to society. I could have been a teacher. I could have been a businessman. I could have done anything worthwhile, but instead I spent two-thirds of my adult life in prison. I have spent a lifetime robbing myself."

Dale Galloway

Echo, Echo, Echo

He that follows the right path shall follow it for his own good, and he that goes astray shall do so at his own peril.

Koran, The Throngs 39:41

"Keep one eye on the law of the echo."

I remember very well the occasion where I first heard this sharp-edged bit of advice. Coming home from boarding school, some of us youngsters were in the dining car of a train. Somehow the talk got around to the subject of cheating on exams, and one boy readily admitted that he cheated all the time. He said that he found it both easy and profitable.

Suddenly a mild looking man sitting all alone at a table across the aisle - he might have been a banker, a bookkeeper, anything - leaned forward and spoke up.

"Yes," he said directly to the apostle of cheating. "All the same - I'd keep one eye on the law of the echo if I were you."

The law of the echo - is there really such a thing? Is the universe actually arranged so that whatever you send out - honesty or dishonesty, kindness or cruelty - ultimately comes back to you? It's hard to be sure. And yet, since the beginning of recorded history, mankind has had the conviction, based partly on intuition, partly on observation, that in the long run a man does indeed reap what he sows.

Arthur Gordon

Each human being is like a rider sitting up in a chariot, driving a team of two horses – a black one and a white one, the good and evil that is in each of us. And that man's job, with the grace of God, is to keep the evil horse from wrecking his chariot.

Plato

Even in the Little Things

I the Lord search the heart, I try the reins, even to give every man according to his ways, and according to the fruit of his doings.

Jeremiah 17:10 KJV

Four young men once competed to become head of the trust department at the bank where they worked. After considering the merits of each applicant, the board of directors made its decision. They decided to notify the young man of his promotion, which included a substantial raise in salary, at a meeting scheduled after lunch.

During the noon hour, the young man they had selected went to the cafeteria for lunch. One of the directors was several people behind him in the line. The director saw the young man select his food and a small piece of butter. As soon as he flipped the butter onto his plate, however, he shuffled some food on top of it to hide it from the cashier. Thus, he avoided paying for it.

That afternoon the directors met to notify the young man of his promotion, but prior to bringing him into the room, the incident was related to the entire board. Rather than give the young man the promotion, they called him in to discharge him from the bank. They had concluded that if he was willing to lie to a cashier about a small bit of butter on his plate, he would be just as willing to lie about what was in the bank's accounts.

God's Little Daily Devotional

God's Circle

I have always thought of coincidences as conclu-sions. For whatever reason, wheels are set in motion and sometimes it takes a long time before the reverberations they set up are felt. I think of it sort of as a boomerang. You throw a boomerang, it goes out, turns around and comes back to where it started. I think coincidences somehow work this way. An action takes place in life and eventually comes full circle, back to where it started.

Chuck Vrtacek

God made the universe on the plan of a circle. While yet people thought that the world was flat, and thousands of years before they found out that it was round, Isaiah inti-mated the shape of it, God sitting upon the circle of the earth. There are in the natural world straight lines, angles, parallelograms, diagonals, quadrangles; but these evidently are not God's favorites. Almost everywhere where you find Him geometrizing you find the circle dominant - the stars in a circle, the moon in a circle, the sun in a circle, the universe in a circle, and the throne of God the center of that circle.

What is true in the material universe is true in God's moral government and spiritual arrangement. That is the meaning of the Prophet Ezekiel's wheel. Commentators agree in saying that the wheel means God's providence. But a wheel is of no use unless it turn, and if it turn it turns around, it moves in a circle. What then? Are we parts of a great iron machine, whirled around whether we will or not, the victims of inexorable fate? No. Far from that, as I shall show you that we ourselves start the circle of good or bad actions, and they will surely come around to us. Those good or bad actions may make the circuit of many years; but come back to us they will as certainly as God sits on the circle of the earth.

Queen Jezebel, the worst woman of the Bible, slew a man named Naboth because she wanted his vineyard. While the dogs were eating the body of Naboth, Elijah the Prophet put down his compass and marked a circle from those dogs clear around to the dogs that would eat the body of Jezebel, the murderess.

"Impossible," the people said; "that will never happen to the Queen." But then, who was that being flung out of the palace window? Jezebel. A few hours later, those who came around, hoping to bury her, found only the palms of her hands and the skull. The dogs had devoured Jezebel, as the dogs had devoured Naboth! Oh, what a swift, what an awful circuit.

Do not become impatient because you cannot see the curve of events, and therefore conclude that God's government is going to break down. Shall we take our little watch, which we have to wind up every night lest it run down, and hold it up beside the clock of the eternal ages? Sometimes it is a wider circle and does not return for a great while, wider and wider, starting other circles, convoluting, over-running, circumscribing, over-arching all of heaven.

But what is true of the good is just as true of the bad. You utter a slander against your neighbor. It has gone forth from your teeth. It will never come back, you think. You have done the man all the mischief you can. You rejoice to see him wince. You say: "Didn't I give it to him?" That word has gone out, that slanderous word, on its poisonous and blasted way. You think it will never do you any harm. But I am watching that word, and I see it beginning to curve, and it curves around, and it is aiming at your heart. You had better dodge it. You cannot dodge it. It rolls into your bosom, and after it rolls in a word from the Good Book says, "With what measure you use, it shall be measured to you again."

You mistreat an aged parent. You begrudge him the room in your house. You are impatient of his whimsicalities. It makes you mad to hear him tell the same story twice. You wish he was away. You wonder if he is going to live forever. He will be gone very soon. His steps are shorter and shorter. He is going to stop. But God has an account to settle with you on that subject. After a while your eye will be dim and your gait will halt, and the sound of the grinding will be slow, and you will tell the same story twice, and your children will wonder if you are going to live forever, and wonder if you will never be taken away. They called you "father" once; now they call you "the old man." What are those rough words with which your children are accosted you? They are the echo of the very words you used in the ear of your old father forty years ago.

We ourselves start the circle of good or bad actions, and they will surely come around to us. Those good or bad actions may make the circuit of many years; but come back to us they will as certainly as God sits on the circle of the earth.

H. S. Smith

I know this world is ruled by Infinite Intelligence.
It required Infinite Intelligence to create it and it requires Infinite Intelligence to keep it on its course.
It is mathematical in its precision.
Thomas Edison

One Good Turn Deserves Another

If you help others, you will be helped, perhaps to-morrow, perhaps in one hundred years, but you will be helped. Nature must pay off the debt. It is a mathematical law and all life is mathematics.

Gurdjieff

The long arm of coincidence reached out and touched the lives of two Texans in one of the strangest series of events ever.

One of the men was Allen Falby, an El Paso County highway patrolman; the other was Alfred Smith, a businessman. They met for the first time on a hot June night when Falby crashed his motorcycle.

He was racing down the road to overtake a speeding truck when the vehicle slowed down to make a turn. Unaware the truck was slowing, Falby slammed full throttle into the tailgate.

The crackup demolished the cycle and nearly amputated one of Falby's legs from his battered body. As he lay in agony on the pavement, a pool of blood began to form beneath his shattered limb. He had ruptured an artery in his leg and was bleeding to death. It was then that fate brought Falby and Smith together.

Smith had been driving home along the road when he saw the accident. Shaken but alert, he was out of his car and bending over the badly injured man almost before the sound of the impact died on the night air.

Smith wasn't a doctor but could see what had to be done for the dying patrolman. Whipping off his tie, Smith quickly bound Falby's leg in a crude tourniquet. It worked. The flow of blood slackened to a trickle and then stopped entirely.

When the ambulance arrived a few minutes later, Smith learned he had saved Falby's life.

Falby was hospitalized for several months. After corrective surgery, he eventually returned to his police job. Five years later, around Christmas, Falby was on highway night patrol when he received a radio call from headquarters to investigate a bad accident along U.S. 80. A car had smashed into a tree. A man was in serious condition, and an ambulance was on the way.

Falby reached the wreck well before the ambulance. Pushing his way past a group of frightened bystanders, he found the injured man slumped unconscious across the torn car seat. The man's right pants leg was saturated and sticky with blood. He had severed a major artery and was bleeding to death.

Well trained in first aid, Falby quickly applied a tourniquet above the ruptured artery. When the bleeding stopped, he pulled the man from the car and made him more comfortable on the ground.

That's when Falby recognized the victim. He was Alfred Smith, the man who had saved his own life five years before. By an incredible coincidence, fate had brought the two men together again - and both meetings had been for the same purpose: for one man to save the life of the other in exactly the same way.

"Well," Falby said, "you might say, it all goes to prove that one good tourniquet deserve another.'"

As cited in *Incredible Coincidence* by Alan Vaughan

Elijah - God's Prophet

Let us not become weary in doing good, for at the proper time we will reap a harvest if we do not give up.
Galatians 6:9

Now Elijah...said to Ahab, "As the Lord, the God of Israel, lives, whom I serve, there will be neither dew nor rain in the next few years except at my word."

Then the word of the Lord came to Elijah: "Leave here, turn eastward and hide in the Kerith Ravine, east of the Jordan. You will drink from the brook, and I have ordered the ravens to feed you there."

So he did what the Lord had told him. He went to the Kerith Ravine, east of the Jordan, and stayed there. The ravens brought him bread and meat in the morning and bread and meat in the evening, and he drank from the brook.

Some time later the brook dried up because there had been no rain in the land. Then the word of the Lord came to him: "Go at once to Zarephath of Sidon and stay there. I have commanded a widow in that place to supply you with food." So he went to Zarephath. When he came to the town gate, a widow was there gathering sticks. He called to her and asked, "Would you bring me a little water in a jar so I may have a drink?" As she was going to get it, he called, "And bring me, please, a piece of bread."

"As surely as the Lord your God lives," she replied, "I

don't have any bread - only a handful of flour in a jar and a little oil in a jug. I am gathering a few sticks to take home and make a meal for myself and my son, that we may eat it - and then die."

Elijah said to her, "Don't be afraid. Go home and do as you have said. But first make a small cake of bread for me from what you have and bring it to me, and then make something for yourself and your son. For this is what the Lord, the God of Israel, says: 'The jar of flour will not be used up and the jug of oil will not run dry until the day the Lord gives rain on the land.'"

She went away and did as Elijah had told her. So there was food every day for Elijah and for the woman and her family. For the jar of flour was not used up and the jug of oil did not run dry, in keeping with the word of the Lord spoken by Elijah.

Some time later the son of the woman who owned the house became ill. He grew worse and worse, and finally stopped breathing.

"Give me your son," Elijah replied. He took him from her arms, carried him to the upper room where he was staying, and laid him on his bed. Then he stretched himself out on the boy three times and cried to the Lord, "O Lord my God, let this boy's life return to him!"

The Lord heard Elijah's cry, and the boy's life returned to him, and he lived. Elijah picked up the child and carried him down from the room into the house. He gave him to his mother and said, "Look, your son is alive!"

I Kings 17:1-17,19, 21-23

Have Faith

Life is something like this trumpet. If you don't put anything into it, you don't get anything out.

Jazzman William Handy

This letter was found in a can wired to the handle of an old pump at the site offering the only possibility of drinking water on a very lonely and seldom-used trail across Nevada's Amargosa Desert. The letter reads:

This pump is all right as of June 1932. I put a new sucker washer into it and it ought to last five years. But the washer dries out and the pump has got to be primed. Under the white rock I buried a bottle of water, out of the sun with the cork end up. There's enough water in it to prime the pump but not if you drink some first. Pour in about one-fourth of the water and let her soak to wet the leather. Then pour in the rest medium fast and pump like hell. You'll git water. The well never has run dry. Have faith.

When you git watered up, fill the bottle and put it back like you found it for the next feller.

SIGNED: *Desert Pete*

P.S. Don't go drinking the water first! Prime the pump with it and you'll git all you can hold. And next time you pray, remember that God is like the pump. He has to be primed. I've given my last dime away a dozen times to prime the pump of my prayers, and I've fed my last beans to a stranger while saying Amen. It never failed yet to git me an answer. You got to git your heart fixed to give before you can be give to.

Bruce Larson

One of my favorite sayings came off a soda bottle:

NO DEPOSIT
NO RETURN

To me that means you'll get out of life about what you're willing to put in.

John Naber

Mercury and the Woodman

I am really old-fashioned and square. I think your chances of coming out OK are better if you do what you think is right. I think that honesty is still the best policy. I think morality still pays off. I believe in all those old-fashioned things because I honestly think they work.

Ann Landers

A poor Woodman was cutting down a tree near the edge of a deep pool in the forest. It was late in the day and the Woodman was tired. He had been working since sunrise and his strokes were not so sure as they had been early that morning. Thus it happened that the axe slipped and flew out of his hands into the pool.

The Woodman was in despair. The axe was all he possessed with which to make a living, and he had not money enough to buy a new one. As he stood wringing his hands and weeping, the god Mercury suddenly appeared and asked what the trouble was. The Woodman told what had happened, and straightway the kind Mercury dived into the pool. When he came up again he held a wonderful golden axe.

"Is this your axe?" Mercury asked the Woodman.

"No," answered the honest Woodman, "that is not my axe."

Mercury laid the golden axe on the bank and sprang back into the pool. This time he brought up an axe of silver, but the Woodman declared again that his axe was just an ordinary one with a wooden handle.

Mercury dived down for the third time, and when he came up again he had the very axe that had been lost.

The poor Woodman was very glad that his axe had been found and could not thank the kind god enough. Mercury was greatly pleased with the Woodman's honesty.

"I admire your honesty," he said, "and as a reward you may have all three axes, the gold and the silver as well as your own."

Honesty is the best policy.

Aesop

The Beggar King

The only way to help ourselves is to help others.
Elie Wiesel

Once there was a time, according to legend, when Ireland was ruled by a king who had no son. The king sent out his couriers to post notices in all the towns of his realm advising every qualified young man to apply for an interview with the king as a possible successor to the throne. However, all such candidates must have these two qualifications: They must (1) love God and (2) love their fellow human beings.

The young man about whom this legend centers saw a notice and reflected that he loved God and, also, his neighbors. One thing stopped him from going to the castle immediately: he was so poor that he had no clothes that would be presentable in the sight of the king. Nor did he have the funds to buy provisions for the long journey to the castle. But the young man finally managed to scrounge enough money for some appropriate clothes and a few necessary supplies.

Properly attired, the young man then set out on his quest, and had almost completed the journey when he came upon a poor beggar by the side of the road. The beggar sat trembling, clad only in tattered rags. His extended arms pleaded for help. His weak voice croaked, "I'm hungry and cold.

Help me, please?"

The young man was so moved by this beggar's need that he immediately stripped off his new clothes and put on the tattered threads of the beggar. Without a second thought he gave the beggar all his provisions as well. Then, somewhat hesitantly, he continued his journey to the castle dressed in the rags of the beggar, lacking provisions for his return trek home.

Upon his arrival at the castle, a king's attendant showed him into the great hall. After a brief respite to clean off the journey's grime, he was finally admitted to the throne room of the king.

The young man bowed low before his majesty. When he raised his eyes, he gasped in astonishment. "It's you!! You are the beggar by the side of the road."

"Yes," the king replied, "I was that beggar."

"But, but, but you are not really a beggar. You are the king! Why, then, did you do this?" the young man stammered after gaining more of his composure.

"Because I had to find out if you genuinely loved God and your fellow human beings," said the king. "I knew that if I came to you as king, you would have been impressed by my golden crown and royal robes. You would have done anything I asked of you because of my regal character. But that way I would never have known what is truly in your heart. So I used a plan. I came to you as a beggar with no claims on you except for the love in your heart. And I discovered that you sincerely do love God and your fellow human beings. You will be my successor," promised the

king. "You will inherit my kingdom."
As cited in *More Sower's Seeds* by Brian Cavanaugh

Practicing the Golden Rule is not a sacrifice, it's an investment.

Byllye Avery

From a Kernel to Abundance

It is one of the most beautiful compensations in life that no man can sincerely try to help another without helping himself.

Ralph Waldo Emerson

My farmer friends expertly capitalize on the principle of geometric progression. For every kernel of corn planted, one stalk will grow. Each stalk then produces an average of two ears of corn, each of which will yield approximately 200 kernels of corn. Of course, these kernels will become 400 stalks of corn, each of which will have a couple of new ears of corn, with a total of 400 kernels. It's phenomenal. In just one season, one ear of corn becomes 160,000 kernels.

I've learned plenty from my farming friends about the value of geometric progression. I've also learned that kindness reproduces itself in the very same way. One unselfish, kind act you do today may very well inspire the kindness of others.

The Bible says, "Be not weary in well doing." Why? That which you sow, you will also reap; that which you send out, comes back; and what you give, you get. An abundance of kindness begins with one simple "kernel."

Glenn Van Ekeren

What I've Learned So Far

Remember that the people on our planet are not standing in a line single file. Look closely. Everyone is really standing in a circle, holding hands. Whatever you give to the person standing next to you eventually comes back to you.
H. Jackson Brown, Jr.

I've learned that the desire to have a positive impact on the life of each person I meet every day has an even bigger impact on my own life. Age 38

I've learned that if I want the circumstances of my life to change for the better, I must change for the better. Age 42

I've learned that a kindness done is never lost. It may take a while, but like a suitcase on a luggage carousel, it will return again. Age 77

I've learned that you shouldn't expect life's very best if you're not giving it your very best. Age 51

I've learned that you can make a dime dishonestly, but that it will cost you a dollar later on. Age 59

I've learned that the best way to cheer up yourself is to cheer up someone else. Age 13

I've learned that you shouldn't go through life with a catcher's mitt on both hands. You need to be able to throw something back. Age 66

I've learned that generous people seldom have emotional and mental problems. Age 51

I've learned that if you want an immediate high, give a homeless person ten dollars. Age 32

I've learned that I feel better about myself when I make others feel better about themselves. Age 18

I've learned that if you are happy, it is because you put others before yourself. Age 86

I've learned that praying for your enemies instead of fighting with them helps both them and you. Age 14

Complete Live and Learn and Pass It On
by H. Jackson Brown, Jr.

Delayed But Not Denied

Give, and it will be given to you...for with the measure you use, it will be measured to you.

Luke 6:38

Have you ever wondered why things end up as they do? Have you ever thought things just happened by chance?

Let's look at the Word and find out the reason things end up as they do.

When we talk about the law of sowing and reaping, we are talking about something that always works. It cannot be denied. It must happen.

In Genesis 8:22, the Bible tells us, *While the earth remaineth, seedtime and harvest, and cold and heat, and summer and winter, and day and night shall not cease.*

That means it is a law - as long as the earth remains.

The apostle Paul states the same thing in Galatians 6:7: *Be not deceived; God is not mocked: for whatsoever a man soweth, that shall he also reap.*

Let's look at some examples in the Word that tell us that what you sow is what you will reap. Job 4:8 says, *Even as I have seen, they that plow iniquity, and sow wickedness, reap the same.* In Exodus 1:22, Pharaoh gave a decree to drown all the male Hebrew babies who were born. In Exodus 14:28, fourteen chapters later, Pharaoh's army was drowned in the Red Sea.

In Judges 1:6, Adonibezek got his thumbs and big toes cut off. In verse 7, Adonibezek stated that he did this to seventy kings.

In Genesis 12 and 20, Abraham said both times that his wife Sarah was his sister and the kings then took her into their harems and bathed her and prepared her to be one of their wives. In Genesis 26:7, Abraham's son, Isaac, did the very same thing with his wife, Rebekah. Deuteronomy 5:9 tells us that the sins of the fathers are passed down to the third and fourth generations. Isaac did the exact thing that his father had done.

Dorcas, in Acts 9, was a woman who was full of almsdeeds (gift giving to the needy.) When she became sick and died, the disciples sent for Peter. Upon his arrival, Peter knelt down and prayed for Dorcas. She opened her eyes and sat up. Dorcas sowed good works and tender mercies toward the saints and widows, and in return, was raised from the dead.

When Elijah went to Zarephath in 1 Kings 17, he saw a widow gathering sticks and asked her to bring him some bread and a cup of water. Although she had only a handful of flour and a little oil, she did as the prophet asked. Sometime later, the widow's son had become sick and died. Elijah told her to give him her son and went to an upper room. Elijah cried out to the Lord for the boy's life. The Lord heard Elijah's prayer, and the life of the child returned to him. Years before, the widow gave to Elijah all she had, and now years later, she was not denied the life of her son.

In the Book of Esther we read how Haman devised a

67

deceitful plan to destroy innocent lives: those of Mordecai and all the Jews with him. But Haman's lies would be under-covered before the innocent lives were taken and it would be Haman who would die on the gallows he himself had built to murder the others.

Acts 10 tells us about the Roman soldier, Cornelius. He was a Gentile who actively sought God, revered Him, and was generous in meeting the needs of people. An angel appeared to him to tell him that his

prayers and charitable giving had come up for a memorial before God. The angel also told Cornelius to send for Simon Peter to come to his house. Peter shared the Gospel with Cornelius' family, and they were filled with the Holy Spirit and then baptized. As Cornelius sowed good things in life, God added to him and his household.

You see, whenever there is sowing, there will be reaping; whenever there is a cause, there is also an effect. This comes out in our lives in many ways.

I think the greatest example of sowing and reaping that the Scriptures reveal is in Luke 6:36-38, *Be ye therefore merciful as your Father also is merciful. Judge not, and ye shall not be judged: condemn not, and ye shall not be condemned: forgive, and ye shall be forgiven: give, and it shall be given unto you; good measure, pressed down, and shaken together, and running over, shall men give into your bosom.*

Friends, in life we will always receive those things which we give. If I'm selfish, then people will be selfish with me. If I give love to others, then I will receive love. If

I give mercy to others, then I will receive mercy. The law of sowing and reaping will never be denied.

May God use you in the lives of others to add value to them so that God may use others to increase you and add value to your life.

Keep sowing good things.

Reverend Robb Thompson

A Chance Encounter

It is not only what we do, but also what we do not do, for which we are accountable.

Moliere

Before he was elected the 25th President of the United States, William McKinley served in Congress. On his way to his congressional office one morning, he boarded a streetcar and took the only remaining seat. Minutes later, a woman who appeared to be ill boarded the car. Unable to find a seat, she clutched an overhead strap next to one of McKinley's colleagues – another congressman who then hid behind his newspaper when he saw the woman and did not offer his seat. McKinley walked up the aisle, tapped the woman on the shoulder, offered her his seat, and took her place in the aisle.

Years later when McKinley was President, the same congressman was recommended to him for a post as ambassador to a foreign nation. McKinley refused to appoint him. He feared a man who didn't have the courtesy to offer his seat to a sick woman in a crowded streetcar would lack the courtesy and sensitivity necessary to be an ambassador in a troubled nation. The disappointed congressman bemoaned his fate to many in Washington, but never did learn why McKinley chose someone else for the position.

God's Little Daily Devotional

Act as if everything you do will make a difference in your life. It will.

William James

A Mysterious Benefactor

*The only people with whom you should try to get
even are those who have helped you.*

Mae Maloo

Once upon a time, in the gentle foothills of America's
Ozark Mountains, there lived a widow. Her home was a
humble farm cabin which she had shared with her husband,
but now she was alone in the world.

One morning toward the hour of noon, three men rode
on horseback into the farmyard. One of the men dismount-
ed and knocked on the cabin door. He explained to the
widow that he and his friends were weary travelers, far from
home, hungry and hankering for a hot home-cooked meal.
Would it be too much trouble . . . that is, would she mind
cooking such a meal for them?

The widow was reticent at first. Still, the strangers did
appear hungry, and they were very polite. So she explained
that there was not much food in the cabin, but they were
welcome to what food she did have.

The men expressed their gratitude. Once inside the
cabin, they were even more deeply touched by the widow's
generosity. It was obvious she was painfully poor. The little
evidences of her lonely struggle to survive were everywhere: the meager furnishings, the supply cabinets mostly
empty. One of the travelers then noticed a tear on the

widow's cheek and asked what was the matter.

She replied that no one but she had eaten at that table since her husband's death. And now, having men in the cabin again, well, it just reminded her of happier times. There was something else, and at this point the widow began to sob.

At four o'clock that very afternoon, she would be without a home. In less than four hours, the man who held the mortgage to her farm would come to foreclose. Eight hundred dollars remained on the mortgage, a hundred times more than she could afford to pay.

The travelers stared at each other in icy, ashamed silence. How could they have imposed upon a woman who was already heaped with such burdens?

When they finished their meal and had thanked the widow for her hospitality, the shadows of mid-afternoon were yawning in the farmyard. One of the men then clasped the widow's hand in parting. "You remind me so much of my own mother," he said. Into her other hand he gently placed a roll of bills. American currency. Eight hundred dollars.

The mysterious benefactor? Jesse James.

Paul Aurandt

A Circle of Happiness

Sometimes when I consider what tremendous consequences come from little things, I am tempted to think there are no little things.

Bruce Barton

I was about four months into starting up my own landscape architecture business when a friend called me in a panic asking if I could help her out. She had a catering operation that was supposed to put on an important luncheon that weekend, and three of her employees had gotten stranded by a snowstorm. My own schedule was stressed enough, but I agreed to help, even though I had no experience as a waiter.

During the luncheon, to my mortification, I spilled half a plate of rice pilaf onto a man's lap. He was very gracious and made some comment about me being new to this kind of thing. Very embarrassed, I confessed that I was actually a landscape architect, more comfortable slinging bags of fertilizer than balancing gourmet delicacies.

Two days later he called me, having tracked me down through the catering company, and asked me to bid on a job landscaping the front of his office. I ended up doing the work, and when the job was finished, I went by to pick up my payment. I saw that he had erected in his front yard a small sign saying "Landscaped by Ross Gardens" with my name and phone number on it. The place was such a showpiece that it launched my career and five years later, I am still getting business from that little sign.

Isn't it amazing how life works? You never know where anything will lead! You take your cousin's daughter to a matinee as a favor and bump into the man you end up marrying. You agree to organize the charity ball for the hospital and meet the heart surgeon who eventually saves a family member's life.

When we extend ourselves to others, we reap not only the peace of mind and satisfaction of having done the right thing, but we place ourselves where we should be - in the flow of our lives, fully open to the next mysterious and surprising turn of fate.

The Practice of Kindness

Heart Gifts

It's not the things that can be bought
that are life's most richest treasure;
It's just the little "heart gifts"
that money cannot measure.

A cheerful smile, a friendly word,
a sympathetic nod;
Are priceless little treasures
from the storehouse of our God.

They are the things that can't be bought
with silver or with gold;
For thoughtfulness and kindness
and love are never sold.

These are the priceless things in life
for which we cannot pay;
And the giver finds rich recompense
in giving them away.

Pam Smith

If you continually give, you will continually have.

Chinese Proverb

Chapter 1 – Summary

Living Our Best Lives

There is only one way to overcome the result of a series of bad choices, and that is through a series of good choices.
Joyce Meyer

The poet Madeline Bridges reminds us, "Give to the world the best you have, and the best will come back to you."

Her poem encourages us to live our lives with honor and purity, with faith and truth, with love and loyalty. Why? Because nobility matters.

The central message to the quotations, stories, and poems shared in the preceding chapter is this: The choices we make today define our tomorrows. When we make the decision to commit ourselves to ethical excellence - and commit ourselves to being true to our best selves - we begin living our best lives. Our own choices usher us into a better place, or our own choices keep us out.

This message is not a new one. In fact, it is as old as time itself. This "doing unto others" and, in turn, experiencing the "cause and effect" result of our own actions is the ruling truth of life. Its wisdom crosses cultures, nations and faiths. The sooner we understand this, the sooner we can begin to use this mathematical measurer of cause and effect to our benefit.

Before we can begin, we must first be willing to take responsibility for our life up until this point and make the determination to continue to do so from this point on. This means owning up to the fact that we have had something to do with where we find ourselves in life right now. This process takes honesty, and it takes courage. It may also take more time to do than one would at first suppose - especially if we have been in the habit of blaming others for our life or in the habit of making excuses.

However, no matter how difficult it is to get serious about this most important first step, it is a step which must be taken. It is only when we understand that our choices - our own choices – are at the root of our blessing, will we be able to move forward in life in a more positive way.

Our lives are made up of, and defined by, moments. Just moments. Think connect-the-dots. Each experience of our life, in and of itself, may seem insignificant, but when added to another experience, and still more others, a picture slowly begins to emerge of who we are and what we have become.

The "big picture" of our life didn't just show up on the scene one day. It emerged. Little by little, choice by choice, we were defining our days and defining our lives. Thus, all those little things were really the big thing.

Do not discount this thought. Do not allow yourself to be fooled into believing that the little things in life are "no big deal." Nothing could be further from the truth. The true examples we just read about the bank executive who lost a promotion over a small piece of butter and the Congressman who lost an Ambassadorship by not offering his seat to an ill lady on a streetcar are real life examples of this principle at work. Each illustrates the fact that when we make the decision to pass over opportunities to be kind, or when we make the decision to pass over our moral responsibility to be honest, then blessings pass over us as well.

Once you've got a handle on the responsibility aspect of this subject, next start paying attention to the details of your life to determine where you stand in terms of ethical excellence. Take a close look at the possible choices you may be making throughout the day that could be affecting your access to blessing.

Here are just a few questions for you to consider:

Do you frequently do personal business on company time? Do you make personal phone calls, send personal e-mails to friends, or use the internet for non-company business while you are suppose to be working?

Do you call in to work from time-to-time and tell your supervisor you are sick when you are feeling just fine and think nothing of it?

Are you entitled to an employee discount at your place of employment and then use this discount on the sly to make purchases for your family and friends, giving them discounts they are not entitled to? If so, stop. All of these activities are "doing unto another" – namely, your employer – a disservice. And when we cheat another person, we cheat ourselves. Resolve to do nothing at your place of employment that you would not do if the owner who signs your paycheck was standing beside you watching. Be worthy of the trust that has been placed in you.

Those who willingly commit themselves to this worthiness – whether it is the trust of their employer, their spouse, their children, or society – experience blessing. It is by being faithful to our truest selves in small ways that we begin living a larger life.

Do you keep your promises? Does your word mean something? Can others count on it? If not, the same disappointment you create in the lives of other people, will find its way into your own.

Do you tell your children to answer the phone and tell the caller you're not home when you are actually sitting right there on the sofa watching TV?

Do you cheat on your taxes?

Do you pay your bills on time or make others wait for the money you owe them? As you make others wait, you will find yourself waiting also for those things entitled to you. Life is a circle, round and round.

Do you readily let a cashier know an error has been made when you are shorted in the amount of change you are suppose to get back, but say nothing when the error is to your benefit? Ethical excellence is exampled by refusing to take that which is not ours. It is exampled in the words, "Excuse me, sir. There seems to be a mistake. I only gave you a ten dollar bill, and you've given me change for a twenty."

How easy it is to be tempted into believing that walking away with an extra ten in our pocket doesn't really matter, but know this: the ten dollars we take dishonestly will evaporate from our lives into thin air – sooner or later – and take another ten with it, this second ten dollars, legitimately belonging to us. Life is a circle, round and round.

Own the power of living life in a virtuous way. Sharpen your conscience. Refuse to live life any longer in the gray areas of rationalization where you talk yourself into doing things you know you shouldn't. Refuse to believe that no one has seen you do those things in secret that you know are wrong. Understand always that someone has seen you, and that someone is you. Get clear on the importance of this person.

This person has the direct power to bless you or withhold everything you hope for. This person holds the power to determine the outcome of your days. This person is the one who sees all and knows all, and who can change it all for the better in a blink of an eye.

We need to get worthy of our own selves and understand that no one is more deserving of our best behavior than we are.

Ethical excellence. Strive for it. Demand it of yourself. Own its power. Then, in giving to the world the best you have, the best *will* come back to you.

CHAPTER 2
Living Lovingly

Love is the Lifter of the Human Soul

Choice, not chance, determines destiny.

E.C. McKenzie

There's an old story that tells of a wise man who was believed to be the wisest person who ever lived. There seemed to be no question he could not answer correctly. So folks came from all around to make inquiries of the ancient sage who dwelled atop a mountain.

Then it happened one day that two mischievous boys climbed the steep pathways that led to the place where the wisest of the wise lived. They, too, had a question they wanted answered, a question they believed would be impossible for the old man to answer correctly. They were quite sure of this.

"Tell me, old man," said the first boy. "Is the bird cupped in my friend's hands dead or alive?"

The old man looked from one boy and then to the other, but said nothing.

"Well, is it dead? Or is it alive?" demanded the second boy who held the bird. "What is the answer?"

The silence of the old man led the boys to believe that they had outsmarted him. But then he spoke. "You wish an answer to your question," replied the old man, "but that which you seek does not lie within *me*, but within *you*. For if I should say to you that the bird is alive, you will crush it to death in an instant, and death will be the final word. But it will be *your* answer, not mine. And if I should say to you that the bird is dead, you will at once unclench your hands where it is now imprisoned, freeing it to flight, and life will be the final word – *yours*, not mine. And so it is *you* who holds the answer, not I."

The boys were speechless, stunned by the perception of this ancient one who could not see into their hands but saw clearly into their hearts.

"Now I say this to you also," continued the old man in a tone of sincerity and compassion. "In your hands you hold your life. You hold the power to crush it or to free it to flight. Remember this always."

Two boys sought out an old man once upon a time seeking an answer to a question concerning a bird, but descended, instead, with an answer concerning their lives. "In your hands," they were told, "you hold the power."

And so it is with us. From the archives of humanity, the Great Truth emerges, again and again, spoken by many voices – by prophets and by princes, by teachers and by preachers – many voices, yet one message: We are the creators or the extinguishers of the light in our lives. Every time we choose to help another instead of hurt, to commend instead of condemn, to share and to care and to be aware of those around us, the light in our life shines brighter. It is this foundational principle that is the essence of our very existence, and it changes not.

When we appreciate and applaud and affirm our fellows, the darkness of our life dispels and light finds its way. But just as surely as this is true, the opposite is also: with every cutting criticism, with every biting word, with every angry outburst, we are spiritually punching at the world around us with invisible clenched fists, and ultimately punching at ourselves, wounding with our words as surely as we would with weapons. And the darkness comes. Let us stop this. It is not the better way.

So, what is? The answer is a simple one: love. Choose it. Choose it now. Choose it always. And it will become increasingly evident as you do so that love is the lifter of the human soul. Our souls can take flight – and will take flight – when we commit to living lovingly.

And how do we do this? The answer, again, is simple. We live lovingly in our words – words like "please" and "thank you" and "That's a great tie!" We live lovingly when we volunteer to coach Little League, or to teach a Sunday School class, or to stock canned goods down at our local food pantry. We live lovingly when we offer to pick up a friend's mail – or babysit their goldfish – because we heard they're going out-of-town. We live lovingly when we pray more for others than we do for ourselves. We live lovingly when we deliver a tin of cookies to a hospital, or to a police station, or to a fire department on Christmas Day. We live lovingly when we give others our undivided attention when they're speaking to us, when we make eye contact, and when we gentle up our tone of voice. We are even living lovingly when we stop to buy a cup of lemonade from the red-headed neighbor boy down the street who just got braces, and when we share the remote control, and when we don't hog the covers.

Livingly lovingly is also about honor and truth and responsibility. We live lovingly when we don't tell the cashier at the movie theater our son is nine and should be charged the discounted price when he's really twelve and a half. We live lovingly when we return our shopping basket to the designated area in the parking lot instead of leaving it stand out in the open where it can roll into someone else's car. We live lovingly when we don't bring eighteen items into the express line marked "up to ten." We live lovingly when we refuse to "help ourselves" to supplies at work that belong to our employer, not to us. We live lovingly when we don't pull into the handicapped parking stall at the mall unless we are.

Livingly lovingly is nothing more, and nothing less, than doing unto others as we wish to be done by. It is simply about taking others into consideration and caring about how our actions will affect them. It is the willingness to ask ourselves how we would feel if we were the owner of the movie theater, or if we were a handicapped person without a place to park, or if we were in the express line with two or three items and were on our way to an appointment behind a fellow with eighteen, or if ours was the car that the shopping basket rolled into.

Living lovingly is about choices. Choices, choices, choices. And when love is the dominating choice of our life, our souls take flight like a little sparrow on a mountaintop did a long, long time ago. Set free.

Ripples

Drop a stone into the water
And in a moment it is gone.
But a hundred ripples
Circle on and on and on.

Share a loving deed of kindness
And in a moment it is gone.
But a hundred ripples
Circle on and on and on.

Say an unkind word to someone
And in a moment it is gone.
But a hundred ripples
Circle on and on and on.

Yes, a hundred ripples
Circle on and on and on.

Cheryl Kirking

We are members one of another; so that you cannot injure or help your neighbor without injuring or helping yourself.

George Bernard Shaw

Appointment With Destiny

In helping others, we shall help ourselves, for what-
ever good we give out completes the circle and comes back
to us.

Flora Edwards

"Chronic renal failure," doctors told my cousin Larry, hooked up to dialysis machines for more than four years but deteriorating rapidly. "Your only hope is a kidney transplant."

I, among several other relatives, was asked to give samples to see if a compatible donor could be found. I readily agreed, without contemplating the consequences. It came as a shock to learn that I was the perfect match.

The call came from the hospital in the middle of my four-year-old daughter's birthday party. My wife, eight months pregnant with our second child, threw me a wary look when I hung up the phone. She had caught the muted conversation, my careful responses. I hadn't wanted to spoil the party, for her sake or my daughter's.

"What is it?" she asked. "Not now," I said, looking pointedly at our child and the birthday cake.

"This is really big, Ronnie," she said, distressed, when our daughter fell asleep later that evening and we withdrew to the kitchen to talk. "Can we think about this for a while?"

"He doesn't have much time, Debra. I told the doctors I

would give them an answer tomorrow."

"*Tomorrow?*" she shrieked. "Do you think the kidney is like an extra tire? What happens when *you* need a spare? Will someone be around to give *you* one?"

"Debra," I said, "this isn't easy for me, either. Believe me, I'm absolutely terrified! And I'm torn. If I'm really honest with myself, I have to admit I would have been vastly relieved to find out I *wasn't* a match. But the fact is that I am."

"Ronnie," Debra said firmly, "this is a *major* surgery, with serious risks involved!"

"Larry is like a brother to me, Deb. It's not something I *want* to do; it's something I *have* to do. What's my life going to be worth if I deny Larry the right to live?"

"This is a *major* decision, Ronnie, one that involves all of us. You have a family now, and a responsibility to this family, too!"

"Debra," I said weakly, "I have to sleep on this."

"I don't want you to do this, Ronnie. I just can't allow you to take the risk!" And she stormed out of the room, her eyes ice cold, her chin set in determination.

Part of me longed to cave in to her demands. I could blame it on her: "So sorry, Larry, but as you know Debra's about to give birth and she just won't allow me to . . ." I envisioned myself saying. But another part of me repudiated that scenario, ashamed.

That night, I tossed and turned in bed in a restless slumber, agonizing over what to do. And then I had a dream. In the dream, I was visiting Larry at the hospital.

I walked in, arranging a cheerful face prior to my entry, and called out in an insincere, hearty manner: "Hey, buddy, how's life?"

"*This* is *not* life," Larry answered. "Can't eat food . . . barely allowed to drink. . . hooked up to the machine for hours, and when the hellish procedure is over, I feel worse than ever."

"But Lar," I interjected, still attempting false cheer. "At least, this procedure lets you move and you're free!"

"Yeah, free!" he replied. "Free to go *to* dialysis and *from* dialysis." He motioned toward the wires hooking him up to the machine. "I'm twenty-eight years old and I've got an umbilical cord that's like a ball and chain!"

"Larry," I said helplessly, "what can I do?"

"I can't go on like this anymore. Help me, please!"

I woke up in a cold sweat. And I resolved, despite my wife's anger and my own misgivings to give him my kidney.

As I was wheeled into the operating room, the doctor at my side murmured some encouragement. "You're in good hands, Ronnie," he said. "You've made a decision you can live with."

The next morning, I woke up groggy and saw a doctor hovering near my side. "Good morning, Ronnie!" he said cheerfully. "How are you feeling aside from the normal postoperative discomfort?" he asked.

"Doc," I groaned, "I don't know what normal is, but I sure am in a lot of pain."

"Yes...well...." He hesitated for a fraction of a second. "I must tell you that something we were not prepared for occurred during the operation."

"What's happened to Larry?" I asked, alarmed.

"He's still on dialysis, but don't worry, we have another match all lined up for him."

I stared at the doctor, confused.

"Ronnie," he began gently, "I doubt that you have ever heard of renal cell carcinoma?" I shook my head no. "It's an incurable form of cancer," he continued, "virtually always fatal."

"Are you saying that Larry has..." I asked tremulously, my heart palpitating, even as the doctor interrupted me in mid-sentence.

"No, Ronnie, he was spared. And so were you. Your ultrasound indicated two healthy kidneys, Ronnie. Either one of them would have saved your cousin. And it was arbitrary, or so we thought, which one we chose to remove. Little did we know that our hands were being guided to the correct one because, Ronnie, once we removed your left kidney, the naked eye was able to see what the ultrasound had failed to show. On the left kidney cortex was a tiny nodule, a nodule of renal cell carcinoma. Had you not elected to donate your kidney to your cousin, you could easily have been dead within a year. And had the kidney not been inspected as thoroughly as it was, Larry would have been dead from *your* cancer."

"Ronnie, your intentions were indeed very noble. You thought you were saving your cousin's life - but as it turns out, my friend, it was Larry who saved *yours*."

Yitta Halberstam and Judith Leventhal

It Will Be Given to You

...whatsoever good thing any man doeth, the same shall he receive of the Lord...

Ephesians 6:8 KJV

Bishop Harry Flynn of Lafayette, Louisiana, was visiting a prison.

As he was leaving, a prisoner asked him for a rosary. The only rosary the bishop had at that moment was a Connemara marble rosary from Ireland in his pocket. Although he hesitated in parting with it, he gave it to the prisoner.

When the bishop returned home, someone was waiting there with a gift for him. When the bishop saw the gift, he couldn't believe his eyes. It was a rosary identical to the one that he had just given the prisoner.

Mark Link

I grew up so poor and was the recipient of so much from so many. I can't give back to those who gave to me, but I can give to others, so I do. And do you know what I've learned? The more I give, the more I have. The stuff just seems to breed in the corners.

Mary E. Webb

Giving and Receiving

Everyone has a story of how another person's act of kindness or understanding – whether large or small – made a tremendous difference in their life. Hearing these stories over and over has made me want to paint a reminder on my wall with this simple message: everything counts. Whatever you say, the way you look or fail to look at another person, the tone of your voice, the noticing of someone else, may take only a moment, may be nothing to you, and yet it may create a miracle in someone else's life.

Dan Wakefield

A public school teacher made clear to me the complex ideas of giving and receiving.

Evidently she noticed something about the way I held the book in reading class and arranged for an eye examination. She did not send me to a clinic; she took me to her own eye doctor, not as a charity case but as a friend. Indeed, I was so intrigued with the activity that I did not realize exactly what had happened until one day at school she gave me the glasses.

"I can't take them. I can't pay for them," I said, embarrassed by my family's poverty.

She told me a story: "When I was a child, a neighbor bought glasses for me. She said I should pay for them someday by getting glasses for some other little girl. So, you see, the glasses were paid for before you were born."

Then the teacher said the most welcome words that anyone had ever said to me: "Someday you will buy glasses for some other little girl."

She saw me as a giver. She made me responsible. She believed I might have something to offer to someone else. She accepted me as a member of the same world she lived in. I walked out of that room, clutching the glasses, not as a recipient of charity, but as a trusted courier.

Billie Davis

Pass It On

I'm going your way;
Let me help you along.

You seem to be tired
And my arms are strong.

I once too was troubled
With problems and grief,

'Til a friend held me closely
And offered relief.

And all that my friend asked
Before he was gone

Was that when I felt better
I should pass his help on.

Anne Brandt

The Farnham Legacy

The effect of one good-hearted person is incalculable.
Oscar Arias

I was a married dental student in the early 80's with a wife and infant daughter. We moved from the West to the Midwest so I could attend school. We had no family in the area and lived a distance from the school. Making ends meet with a limited income was a challenge, and setting aside money with which to cover medical expenses was almost impossible.

Then our daughter became ill. She had four ear infections in as many months. A couple of times we used money we had received from our parents for a special occasion to cover these expenses.

While I was conversing with a fellow dental student about my problems, he told me of a local pediatrician who treated the children of dental students at no charge. He told me whom to contact and gave me the phone number. This wonderful man, Dr. Paul Farnham, Jr. took care of our daughter and also our second girl born two years later.

That semester, I learned of a fellow dental student whose daughter contracted bronchitis and required immediate medical treatment in order to avoid the risk of pneumonia. He called Dr. Farnham on a Saturday evening. Even though the doctor had been on his way to the symphony, he came into the office and treated the little girl. When my friend offered to pay him, the payment was refused. Instead Dr. Farnham suggested that in the future my friend could do the same for someone else.

Dr. Farnham died suddenly during my third year of dental school. It was at his funeral that the reason for his kindness was revealed. His own father, Dr. Paul Farnham, Sr., had been a married dental student with children and a kind doctor had provided free medical care for his family during the school years. The only thing the other doctor asked was that someday he could help someone else as he had been helped.

I am sure the younger Dr. Farnham repaid the kindness shown his father a hundredfold by caring for the children of dental students for many years. We have always remembered him and try to continue his wonderful legacy.

Bert F. Engstrom, DMD

Androcles Revisited

The kindness we extend to others in their hour of
weakness will return to us at the time we most need.

Amish Proverb

A century ago, not quite forty miles from the city of Paris, was the Forest of Fontainebleau. That resplendent woodland was a Mecca for young artists in search of subject matter, a magical place of pure inspiration where friendly deer nuzzled passersby and undisturbed foliage grew up in grand design. There, as nowhere else on earth, playful lights and shadows teased the eye.

Among the enthralled artistic pilgrims was an aspiring painter in his early twenties, Pierre. Many times Pierre made the two day walk from Paris to the Forest of Fontainebleau just to set up his easel and canvas in the quiet.

One day the woods were more quiet than usual. The birds were silent; the deer did not come as often as before to beg a crust of bread or to watch Pierre's brush in ballet. Soon Pierre learned why: There was a stranger in the glade, a dazed, ragged, mud-spattered stranger stumbling through the tall grass as though he had been pursued by the devil himself.

A desperate voice called to Pierre, shattering the stillness. "Please help me!" it said. "I am dying of hunger!" The intruder fairly collapsed at the young artist's feet.

101

Between gulps of water and bread his story unfolded.

His name was Raoul Rigaud. He was a journalist who had opposed in print France's authoritarian government, and now he was being hunted by imperial authorities. It had been a narrow escape. They had surprised him at his apartment; he had made it out a window and to the balcony of an apartment adjoining his - through that window and down a flight of stairs and into the street and onto a departing train. It had all happened so fast!

Next thing he knew Raoul was wandering through a forest, the Forest of Fontainebleau. He was exhausted, starving. He would give himself up.

Pierre listened sympathetically.

No, declared the young artist, Raoul would not surrender to the authorities! He would stay right there in the woods and wait while Pierre fetched a disguise. There was a village nearby. Pierre would find an artist's smock and a painting kit, and before sundown Raoul Rigaud would be just another artist visitor to the Forest of Fontainebleau.

Raoul remained at Pierre's side for several weeks until the journalist's friends in Paris could be notified. The friends then made arrangements for Raoul to flee France safely.

The parting of Pierre and Raoul was bittersweet. Tears of gratitude filled the fugitive's eyes as he shook Pierre's hand for the last time. "Had it not been for you..." he started to say. Then he turned, and was gone.

A number of years passed. Now it was the spring of 1871. Only weeks before, Napoleon III had been officially deposed; the revolutionary Commune had seized power in

Paris. Pierre, just thirty, was in Paris too. He was painting on the banks of the Seine one day when some national guardsmen stopped to look at his work. The soldiers were quiet at first, but as Pierre continued to paint he heard them muttering to each other. Suddenly one of the soldiers snatched Pierre's unfinished canvas from its easel. Pierre was fooling no one, the guardsman said; Pierre was a spy for the Versailles forces and this so-called painting was proof!

But it *was* a painting, Pierre protested. What possible threat could a mere painting pose to the Paris Commune?

The soldier's gaze was stern. "What do you see here?" he asked his comrades, thrusting Pierre's canvas before them. "A picture, yes—but a picture of what?"

Another guardsman spoke up: obviously it was a secret plan, a diagram of the Seine area showing vulnerable points and strategic locations to guide the Versailles troops.

"An aid to the enemy!" shouted another.

By now a small crowd had gathered on the river bank. Who was this Pierre? They wanted to know. A spy for Versailles? Then throw him in the Seine! Drown him!

But Communard "law" provided for a more orderly disposal of spies. The soldiers placed Pierre under arrest, led him off down the street toward the town hall of the Sixth Arrondissement. There a firing squad was on permanent duty to handle such matters.

The angry crowd followed, crying out for Pierre's death. Within a hundred steps their numbers had increased to mob proportions. "Kill him!" they shouted in terrifying cadence. "Kill him!"

At the vortex of this human maelstrom was poor Pierre. He was not a spy. He was but a young artist trying to make his way in life—and soon, it seemed, his way was to end.

At the town hall Pierre's trial and conviction proved little more than a nod from the captain in charge. Down in the square the firing squad waited, the mob chanted. As Pierre was being led, his hands bound behind him, to the place where he was to die, he returned in his mind to the Forest of Fontainebleau. He patted the grazing deer and watched the sunlight dance. If this world were to pass, perhaps the next would be more like that one in his secret heart.

But when Pierre opened his eyes it was not to see a line of raised rifles. It was to see the Communard Public Prosecutor pushing his way through the crowd. He was a grand sight indeed, dressed in full uniform with tricolor sash, and the soldiers in his attendance were equally magnificent. Moments later the Public Prosecutor and Pierre were standing face to face. "Surely you remember me!" said the Prosecutor, and he embraced the young artist.

The high Communard official who had just happened to be passing was none other than Raoul Rigaud, the onetime political fugitive whom Pierre had rescued in the Forest of Fountainebleau. The attitude of the onlookers inverted at the sight of Raoul's embrace, and a great cheer came forth from the crowd.

Raoul demanded Pierre's release, after which he escorted the young artist to the town hall balcony overlooking the square. "Let us sing the 'Marseillaise' for our comrade!" cried Raoul. And the people sang.

Pierre was given a pass to travel and to paint wherever he wished, and as his adventure drew to a close, life began anew.

Once upon a time, according to legend, there was a Roman slave named Androcles who pulled a thorn from a lion's paw. Later sentenced to death, Androcles met that same lion in the arena. Out of gratitude, the hungry beast refused to devour Androcles, and the slave's much-impressed captors set him free. Pierre felt that this was a real-life re-enactment of that ancient story.

For it was a moment of thoughtfulness, a good deed, which acted indirectly upon his destiny, which blossomed to bestow upon the whole world a genius that might otherwise have consigned itself to oblivion - the fathomless depths of shadow and light, the everlasting art of "Pierre" Auguste *Renoir*, one of the greatest painters ever whose life was spared in Paris.

Paul Aurandt

When you are good to others, you are best to yourself.

Benjamin Franklin

How Could I Miss, I'm a Teacher!

We cannot hold a torch to light another's path without brightening our own.

Ben Sweetland

In the early 1960s in New York City, I worked with a group of eighth and ninth grade students who were only reading at the second to third grade level. I found it difficult not to experience despair as I worked with them, trying to tutor kids who had basically given up on school. Their attendance was spotty at best. I believe many of them came to school simply because that was where most of their friends were that day, rather than because they thought they might learn something.

Attitudinally, they were a disaster. Anger, cynicism, sarcasm and the expectation of being failed, ridiculed or put down was the tenor and content of their talk. I tried to tutor them in small groups and one-on-one, and I must confess the results were not encouraging with most. Oh, there were a few who seemed to respond more positively on an occasional basis, but it was impossible to tell when that marginally positive attitude might disappear, to be replaced by sullenness or unaccountable flashes of anger.

One of my other problems was the fact that, at the time, almost no age-appropriate remedial reading materials were available for junior high school students at such a low level.

They wanted to read about relationships, dating, sports and cars, not materials like "Run, Spot, run! See the ball. It is bouncing." The kids regarded the materials I had as too babyish and beneath them. Unfortunately, more interesting materials were way too difficult in reading level for them to handle without much frustration. Several of them complained continuously about the material. Jose, a tall, lanky boy with a pronounced accent, captured the essence when he said, "Hey, man, this stuff is boring. And it's dumb, too! Why do we got to read this junk, man?"

A glimmer of an idea crept into my mind and so I sought help from my department chairman on how to write a proposal for funding a little tutoring project. We didn't get a huge sum of money, but it was enough for a pilot program for the last six months of the school year. It was simple and it worked.

I "hired" my students as reading tutors. I told them that the nearby elementary school had students in the first, second and third grades who needed help in reading. I had some money that I could pay to anyone who'd help me work with these children. My students asked whether this would take place during or after school.

"Oh, during school. In fact, it will be instead of our class period together. We'll just walk over there each day and work with the kids there.

"You've got to know, that if you don't show up, you don't get paid. And you also have to understand that it would be very disappointing to a young child if you were his or her tutor and you didn't show up or if you didn't work caringly with that child. You'll have a big responsibility!"

All but one of my 11 students jumped at the chance to be a part of this program. The lone holdout changed his mind within one week as he heard from the other students how much they were enjoying working with these young kids.

The elementary kids were grateful for the help but even more so for some attention from these older kids from their own neighborhood. Clearly you could see a version of hero worship in their eyes. Each of my students was assigned two or three younger children to work with. And they worked, reading to them and having them read aloud as well.

My goal was to find a way to legitimize eighth and ninth-graders reading such young material. I thought that, if I could get them to read that material and read regularly, they would surely improve. As it turned out, I was right. At the end of that year, testing showed almost all of them had improved one, two or even three grade levels in reading!!

But the most spectacular changes were in my students' attitudes and behavior. I hadn't expected that they would start to dress better, with more care and more neatness. Nor had I expected that the number of fights would decrease while their attendance dramatically increased.

One morning, as I was entering school from the parking area, I saw Jose walking toward the door. He looked ill. "What's the matter, Jose?" I said, "You look like you might have a fever."

"Oh, I guess I'm feeling kind of sick, Mr. McCarty," he replied.

"So why are you here today? Why didn't you stay

home?" I asked.

His answer floored me. "Oh, man, I couldn't miss today. I'm a *teacher*! My students would miss me, wouldn't they?"

He grinned and went in the building.

Hanoch McCarty

The Man Who Missed Christmas

Love and you shall be loved, for all love is mathematically just – as much as the two sides of an algebraic equation.

Ralph Waldo Emerson

It was Christmas Eve, and, as usual, George Mason was the last to leave the office. He walked over to a massive safe, spun the dials, swung the heavy door open. Making sure the door would not close behind him, he stepped inside.

A square of white cardboard was taped just above the topmost row of strongboxes. On the card a few words were written. George Mason stared at the words written there, remembering . . .

Exactly one year ago he had entered this same vault. And then, behind his back, slowly, noiselessly, the ponderous door swung shut. He was trapped—entombed in the sudden and terrifying dark.

He hurled himself at the unyielding door, his hoarse cry sounding like an explosion. Through his mind flashed all the stories he had heard of men found suffocated in time-vaults. No time-clock controlled this mechanism; the safe would remain locked until it was opened from the outside tomorrow morning. Then the realization hit him. No one would come tomorrow—tomorrow was Christmas.

Once more he flung himself at the door, shouting wildly, until he sank on his knees exhausted. Silence came, high-pitched, screaming silence that seemed deafening. More than 36 hours would pass before anyone came—36 hours in a steel box three feet wide, eight feet long, seven feet high. Would the oxygen last? Perspiring and breathing heavily, he felt his way around the floor. Then, in the far right-hand corner, just above the floor, he found a small, circular opening. Quickly he thrust his finger into it and felt, faint but unmistakable, a cool current of air. The tension release was so sudden that he burst into tears. But at last he sat up. Surely he would not have to stay trapped for the full 36 hours. Somebody would miss him.

But who? He was unmarried and lived alone. The maid who cleaned his apartment was just a servant; he had always treated her as such. He had been invited to spend Christmas Eve with his brother's family, but children got on his nerves, and expected presents.

A friend had asked him to go to a home for elderly people on Christmas Day and play the piano – George Mason was a good musician. But he had made some excuse or other; he had intended to sit at home, listening to some new recordings he was giving himself.

George Mason dug his nails into the palms of his hands until the pain balanced the misery in his mind. Nobody would come and let him out. Nobody, nobody.

Miserably the whole of Christmas Day went by, and the succeeding night. On the morning after Christmas the head clerk came into the office at the usual time, opened the safe, then went on into his private office. No one saw George

Mason stagger out into the corridor, run to the water cooler, and drink great gulps of water. No one paid any attention to him as he left and took a taxi home.

There he shaved, changed his wrinkled clothes, ate breakfast and talked to his own brother. Grimly, inexorably, the truth closed in on George Mason. He had vanished from human society during the great festival of brotherhood; no one had missed him at all.

Reluctantly, George Mason began to think about the true meaning of Christmas. Was it possible that he had been blind all these years with selfishness, indifference, pride? Wasn't giving, after all, the essence of Christmas because it marked the time God gave His own Son to the world?

All through the year that followed, with little hesitant deeds of kindness, with small, unnoticed acts of unselfishness, George Mason tried to prepare himself . . .

Now, once more, it was Christmas Eve.

Slowly he backed out of the safe and closed it. He touched its grim steel face lightly, almost affectionately, and left the office.

There he goes now in his black overcoat and hat, the same George Mason as a year ago. Or is it? He walks a few blocks, then flags a taxi, anxious not to be late. His nephews are expecting him to help them trim the tree. Afterwards, he is taking his brother and his sister-in-law to a Christmas play. Why is he so happy? Why does his bumping into others as he walks, laden as he is with bundles, exhilarate and delight him?

Perhaps the card has something to do with it, the card he

taped inside his office safe last New Year's Day.

On the card is written, in George Mason's own hand: *To love people, to be indispensable somewhere, that is the purpose of life. That is the secret of happiness.*

J. Edgar Park

Joy comes not to him who seeks it for himself, but to him who seeks it for other people.

H. W. Sylvester

The Sin of Omission

It isn't the thing you do, dear,
It's the thing you leave undone,
That gives you a bit of a heartache
At the setting of the sun.

The tender word forgotten,
The letter you did not write,
The flowers you did not send, dear,
Are your haunting ghosts at night.

The stone you might have lifted
Out of a brother's way;
The bit of heartsome counsel
You were hurried too much to say;

The loving touch of the hand, dear,
The gentle, winning tone,
Which you had no time nor thought for
With troubles enough of your own.

Those little acts of kindness
So easily out of mind,
Those chances to be angels
Which we poor mortals find –

They come in night and silence,
Each sad, reproachful wraith,
When hope is faint and flagging,
And a chill has fallen on faith.

For life is all too short, dear,
And sorrow is all too great,
To suffer our slow compassion
That tarries until too late;

And it isn't the thing you do, dear,
It's the thing you leave undone,
Which gives you a bit of a heartache
At the setting of the sun.

Margaret E. Sangster

A Giving Tree

What you deny to others will be denied to you.
Thaddeus Golas

There is an old tale about an unusual tree that grew outside the gates of a desert city. It was an ancient tree, a landmark, as a matter of fact. It seemed to have been touched by the finger of God, for it bore fruit perpetually. Despite its old age, its limbs were constantly laden with fruit. Hundreds of passersby refreshed themselves from the tree, as it never failed to give freely of its fruit.

But then a greedy merchant purchased the property on which the tree grew. He saw hundreds of travelers picking the fruit from "his" tree, so he built a high fence around it. Travelers pleaded and pleaded with the new owner, "Share the fruit with us."

The miserly merchant scoffed, "It's my tree, my fruit, and bought with my money."

And then an astonishing thing happened - suddenly, the ancient tree died! What could have happened?

The law of giving, as predictable as the law of gravity, expresses the immutable principle: When giving ceases, bearing fruit ceases with it.

As cited in *Sower's Seeds of Encouragement* by Brian Cavanaugh

Silas Peterman's Investment

You serve yourself best when you serve others most.

B. C. Forbes

The little girl in the faded dress trudged determinedly down the road. In one hand she carried a pail of blackberries; with the other she twisted and untwisted a string of her pink sunbonnet. She wore no shoes or stockings, but under the pink sunbonnet a pair of steady blue eyes looked out upon the world, undaunted by many hardships. Myrtilla Lucy was not a stranger to them.

All at once she stopped, set down her pail of berries, and looked away in the direction of a large, gray stone building that stood out against the sky on a distant hilltop. Her blue eyes gleamed, her lips parted in a smile, revealing even rows of teeth as white as seed pearls. She drew a long breath.

"It looks good, that school does," she whispered. "Oh, if I could only go there and learn things; I'm praying, praying that I can."

She stood there a moment longer gazing at the stone building gilded by the splendor of a summer's sun. Then she picked up her pail and walked on. Once more she stopped; this time to examine a stone bruise on her foot, but she was soon trudging bravely on again in spite of pain and weariness. She came at last into the town, with its beautiful residences, its wide streets, its well-kept lawns. At the largest and most imposing of these residences she stopped, climbed the stone steps leading to the broad walk, marched up to the large porch, and knocked at the massive door.

A moment later, a white-capped maid opened the door. When she saw the barefooted little girl in the faded dress, she frowned.

"If you have anything to sell, you should go around to the back door," she said sharply. "No one but callers come here."

The little girl pushed back the sunbonnet from her forehead.

"I ain't got anything to sell, and I'm a caller, too," she answered with a certain childish dignity. "I've come to see Mr. Peterman."

The maid stared. "Lord, child," she cried, "you ain't got no kind of a chance to see Mr. Peterman. He's the busiest man in town. He hasn't time to spend on little girls like you."

The child's eyes suddenly filled with tears. "But I've walked eight miles," she said, resolutely winking back the tears. "I've brought him these blackberries, too, and I must see him. I can't - " her lips set themselves in firm and sudden lines - "I can't go home until I do see him."

The maid looked at her again, at the weary little figure; the bare, dusty, small feet; the determined gleam of the blue eyes.

"Well, wait a minute," she said not unkindly, "and I'll see what Mr. Peterman says."

A moment later she came out.

"You can come in," she announced briefly. The little girl followed the maid through a wide and spacious hall into another room where a man sat busy with some papers at a table. He had gray hair, sharp, shrewd eyes, and strong, rugged features. There was a stern, sad look on his face, as if he seldom smiled. He lifted his head when the two came in. The maid spoke.

"This is the little girl, Mr. Peterman."

Silas Peterman pushed away his papers.

"Well," he said, as the maid turned away, "what is it you want with me?"

The little girl came nearer. "May I sit down, sir?" she asked in a sweet, clear voice. "You see, I've walked a long way, and once I bruised my foot on a stone in the road."

"What did you take such a long walk for?" he demanded gruffly. "There, sit down, then."

The little girl took the chair he indicated, still keeping the pail of berries by her side.

"I wanted to see you," she said simply.

"To see me? What for?"

The little girl looked back at him gravely.

"I wanted to ask you," she began slowly, "if you wouldn't send me to that school for girls on the hill yonder. Folks tell me you've got heaps of money, and I thought maybe, when I explain things to you, you wouldn't mind having me for an investment."

"An investment?" cried Silas Peterman.

The little girl nodded. "Yes, an investment. You see, sir, I've always wanted to learn, but at home I haven't any chance. Mother has five others besides me; and Dad, he can't do much, 'count of his poor health. I thought if I could get you to send me to school, why, when I did get educated, maybe I could do something for you. I ain't got no kind of a chance the way things are, so I picked these berries and brought 'em to you for a little present, and I made up my mind I'd come out honest and ask you to send me to that school. Nobody knows I come, not even Mother."

Silas Peterman stared at the small, shabby figure, too astonished to speak.

"What has made you come to me?" he demanded after a bit of silence.

The little girl sighed.

"There wasn't anyone else to come to," she replied. "I don't know of anyone that's got any money except you. I heard Dad tell Mother how rich you were, and you never put any money into anything that wasn't a good investment. And then, I thought I'd come and tell you that I'd be a good investment myself. I'm little now but I'll grow, and maybe when I'm grown you'll be glad you helped me. You never can tell what will happen in this world. Oh, sir, please send me to school and let me learn. I'll pay it back, truly I will. When you get old, I'll come and take care of you if you need anyone; but please, please send me to school. The world is just full of things I don't know about. To go without an education is most as bad as being blind! When you don't know anything, you can't see with your mind. It's all dark. You understand what I mean, don't you?"

Silas Peterman continued to study the small, earnest

face.

"That's a new thought," he answered, "about the mind being blind if one isn't educated. And so," he added reflectively, "you came to me to ask for help, and you brought me some blackberries in that pail, did you?"

"Yes, sir, the finest I could pick. It was all I could do for you, but I think you'll like 'em. They make good pies." She lifted the pail of shining blackberries and placed it on the library table. There was a long silence.

"Well," said Silas Peterman at last, "I am inclined to accept you as an investment. I'm going to give you a chance. It rests on you whether you make good or not."

The little girl in the faded dress sprang up.

"You won't be sorry," she cried. "I'll learn everything I can, and some day I'll do things for you..."

****

"Well," said Mr. Silas Peterman to the president of the school one day, "how is that little girl I sent you last fall doing? Is there anything to her?"

The president smiled. He was a portly gentleman with kind eyes. "Yes, there is a great deal to her," he replied. "She's the brightest girl we have. She's at the head of all her classes. She leaves nothing unlearned that comes her way." He hesitated. "May I ask how it came that you decided to educate her?" he said.

"Well," replied Mr. Peterman, smiling at the memory, "I'll tell you. I did it for an investment."

****

It was twelve years later. The physician looked grave as

he studied his patient.

"Mr. Peterman," he said finally, "you need a change, a trip, a long rest; but someone will have to go with you. Don't you know anyone - some capable young woman upon whom you could depend; someone who would keep things cheerful, and see to your meals and your medicine? Think, now; among all the young people you know surely there is someone."

Silas Peterman shook his head. He looked shrunken and sad as he sat there.

"Who wants to cheer up a crabby old invalid?" he replied. "What young person would be willing to devote her time to a sick man? I haven't anyone related to me to look after me, and I wouldn't ask it of her if I had. We'll say no more about it."

Just at that moment the door opened and a young lady entered. She was slender, erect, and blue eyed - the very vision of health and hope and happiness.

"I've just heard of your illness, Mr. Peterman," she began, as she went forward to greet him. "I came on the first train."

Silas Peterman looked up. A smile broke all over the thin, worn face.

"If it isn't Myrtilla Lucy!?" he said. "But what," he added, "have you done with your schooling?"

"Nobody can take care of you as I can. I'm going to stay for as long as you need me."

The physician's face immediately lost its anxious look. "Just the thing," he said approvingly. "And may I ask, sir," he added, turning to Silas Peterman, "who this young lady is?"

But it was Myrtilla Lucy who answered. She glanced down the vista of years and saw herself a small, ragged, barefooted girl, with her pail of blackberries in her hand. She saw the friend who had opened the magic doors of education to her and given her an entrance into that wider world. She owed everything to that sick, lonely old man in the invalid's chair opposite, and she did not forget it. Suddenly she bent forward and took Silas Peterman's hand, and pressed it lovingly between her two young, firm ones. Her turn had come. She looked at the physician.

"Did you not know," she said gayly, "that over twelve years ago Mr. Peterman made an investment? He took a little ragged girl out of a log cabin and sent her to school. I am that investment."

But it was Silas Peterman who spoke this time. He, too, looked down the long years, and saw Myrtilla Lucy as she had looked that August day, with her bare feet and faded dress, her eager blue eyes. She had told him then that some day he might need her. A great wave of thankfulness rolled over his heart. He wasn't alone any longer. After all, he had someone to lean on. The little bare-footed girl in the faded dress had made good. He turned to his physician. "Yes," he said, and his voice trembled, "she is an investment - and the best one I ever made!"

Susan Huffner Martin

So many of us want peace of mind but do nothing to create it; want love but do not commit loving acts. Kindness, love, compassion, and all the other affirmative values we desire in our lives don't just happen to us; they are generated by our decision to cultivate them within ourselves and then share them with others. If we nourish them, tend them with care, and freely give of them to others, then – and only then – will our lives be full of the positive attributes we long for.

The Practice of Kindness

What Constitutes Quality Human Relationships?

Do as you would be done by.
Persian Proverb

For thousands of years, people have been speculating on what constitutes quality human relationships. With all the philosophies, theories, and speculations, only one principle seems to stand strong. It is not new at all. In fact, it is almost as old as history itself.

It was taught in Persia over three thousand years ago by Zoroaster to his fire worshipers.

Confucius asserted the principle in China twenty-four centuries ago.

In the Valley of Han lived the followers of Taoism. Their leader Lao-tzu taught the principle incessantly.

Five hundred years before Christ, Buddha taught it to his disciples on the banks of the holy Ganges River.

The collections of Hinduism contained this principle over fifteen hundred years before Christ.

Nineteen centuries ago, Jesus taught his disciples and followers much the same principle. He summed it up in one thought: "Do to others as you would have them do to you (Luke 6:31 NIV)."

Glenn Van Ekeren

The Golden Rule

One should seek for others the happiness one desires for one's self.

Buddhist

What you do not want done to yourself, do not do to others.

Confucius

Let none of you treat his brother in a way he himself would not like to be treated.

Muslim Proverb

We should behave to our friends as we would wish our friends to behave to us.

Aristotle, Greek

The law imprinted on the hearts of all men is to love the members of society as themselves.

Roman Proverb

What is hateful to you, do not do to your neighbor. That is the whole Torah.

Hillel, Jewish Rabbi

Deal with others as thou wouldst thyself be dealt by.

The Mahabharata, Hindu

Perfect Timing

For it is in giving that we receive.
Saint Francis of Assisi

The man's name was Roman Turski. Before World War II, Turski was a flight instructor in France. When trouble began to increase throughout Europe, Turski decided to return home to Poland in his small plane. He quit his job and started off, but as he approached Vienna, Austria, his plane developed mechanical trouble. Turski landed, left his plane to be repaired, and went to a hotel for the night.

The next morning as he was leaving his hotel room, Turski was sent reeling by a collision with a man who was running down the hall. Angered, Turski grabbed the man and was about to tell him off when he saw the man's face was white with fear.

"Gestapo! Gestapo!" the man cried.

Turski did not know much German, but he did know what Gestapo meant. The man was running away from the German secret police, and that was very serious. Turski quickly pushed the man, who was small in stature, into his room and closed the door. He motioned for the man to get into his bed, get under the covers, and lie still. Turski arranged the covers so it appeared as if he were arising. He pulled off his jacket, tie, and shirt and sat on the edge of the bed. In a few moments the Gestapo knocked at his door as he expected. They came into the room, examined his passport, returned it and then proceeded to shout questions to him in German. Turski replied with one of the few German phrases he knew. It meant "I don't know." The Gestapo left without searching his room.

When the Gestapo left, the little man crawled out from under the covers, thanking Turski profusely in German. Turski got out his flight chart and by drawing pictures on the margin managed to explain to the stranger that he could fly him out of Austria. But as his destination was Warsaw, he could not take him there. The airport would be filled with police who would arrest him. Turski indicated that he would land in a field just over the Polish border where the man could get off before Turski went on to Warsaw.

Turski managed to do this. When he let the man out of the plane, he gave him most of his money and watched him walk rapidly into the woods.

The police were at the airport when Turski arrived and just as he expected, they searched his plane. When the police were satisfied that no one had been stowed aboard, Turski asked them why they were looking for the man. What had he done? "He's a Jew," the police said.

Soon afterward the war came to Poland. Turski escaped to England where he joined the British Royal Air Force.

One day as Turski was returning to England from a war mission, his plane was hit. He crash-landed just after crossing the English channel. When rescue workers pulled Turski from the plane, he was more dead than alive. The doctors in the hospital to which he was taken hesitated to operate because they did not think he would survive.

Later, when Turski finally awoke enough to recognize people around him, he saw a narrow face with large brown eyes looking down at him.

"Remember me?" the man looking down at him asked. "You once saved my life in Vienna." There was now only a slight German accent.

"How did you find me?" Turski asked, remembering who the man was.

"It's a long story," the man said. "After you dropped me off in the field near the border, I made my way to Warsaw where a friend helped me escape to Scotland. I later found out that you were in the Royal Air Force."

"How did you know my name?" Turski asked.

"I saw it written on the corner of the map you used when we left Austria. I remembered it." Then the man reached over and took Turski's wrist. "Yesterday I read the story in the newspaper about a Polish hero shooting down five enemy planes in one day before crash-landing near this hospital. It said your condition was hopeless. I immediately asked the Royal Air Force to fly me to this hospital."

"Why?" Turski asked.

"I thought I could do something to show my gratitude," the man said. "You see, I am a brain surgeon, and I operated on you this morning."

Roman Turski

If you don't look out for others, who's gonna look out for you?

Whoopi Goldberg

We Will Meet Again

We must not, in trying to think about how we can make a big difference, ignore the small daily differences we can make, which, over time, add up to big differences that we often cannot foresee.

Marion Wright Edelman

During the Roosevelt era, times were tough. The president was promising a brighter moon, but the Beasley family hadn't seen it rise over their small town in the Texas panhandle.

So when the call came that their son was ill in California, Bill Beasley didn't know how he was going to scrape together the money for his wife and himself to make the trip.

Bill had worked as a trucker his entire life, but he never managed to accumulate any savings. Swallowing his pride, he phoned a few close relatives for help, but they were no better off.

So it was with embarrassment and dejection that Bill Beasley walked the mile from his house to the filling station and told the owner, "My son is pretty sick," he said, "and I've got no cash. Can you trust me for a phone call to California?"

"Pick up the phone and talk as long as you need to," was the reply.

As Mr. Beasley started to dial, he was interrupted by a

voice asking, "Aren't you Bill Beasley?"

It was a stranger, jumping down from the cab of a truck with out-of-state plates. The young man didn't look familiar, and Bill could only stare at him with a puzzled look and say, "That's right, I am."

"Your son was one of my best pals when we were growing up together, remember? When I went off to college, I lost all track of him." He paused for a moment and then continued. "Heard you say he's sick?"

"Kinda bad from what we hear. I'm gonna call and try to make some arrangements for the wife to get out there to be with him."

Then, as a matter of courtesy, Mr. Beasley told the trucker, "Have yourself a Merry Christmas, young man," then paused and added, "I wish your daddy was still with us. I miss him."

Old man Beasley walked into the office of the station and placed his call to the West coast, informing his boy that he or his wife hoped to be out as soon as possible.

There was an obvious look of sorrow on the elder citizen's face as he assured the owner that he would pay for the call as soon as he could.

"The call has been paid for. That trucker - the one your son used to pal around with - left me a twenty dollar bill and said to give you the change when the phone bill comes in. He also left you this envelope."

The old man fumbled open the envelope and pulled out two sheets of paper. One read, "You were the first trucker I ever traveled with, Mr. Beasley, the first one my dad trusted enough to let me go along with when I was barely five years old. I remember you bought me a Snickers bar."

The second sheet, much smaller in size, was a signed check with an attached message: "Fill out the amount needed for you and your wife to make the trip to California. And give your son, my pal, a Snickers bar. Merry Christmas!"

Author Unknown

The Golden Rule Revisited

Whatever path of action you find that brings good and happiness to all, follow this way like the moon in the path of the stars.

Indian Proverb

They lie there, breathing heavy gasps, contracted into a fetal position. Ironic, that they should live 80 or 90 years, then return to the posture of their childhood. But they do. Sometimes their voices are mumbles and whispers like those of infants or toddlers. I have seen them, unaware of anything for decades, crying out for parents long since passed away.

I recall one who had begun to sleep excessively, and told her daughter that a little girl slept with her each night. I don't know what she saw. Maybe an infant she lost, or a sibling, cousin or friend from years long gone. But I do know what I see when I stand by the bedside of the infirm aged. Though their bodies are skin-covered sticks and their minds an inescapable labyrinth, I see something surprising. I see something beautiful and horrible, hopeful and hopeless. What I see is my children, long after I leave them, as they end their days.

This vision comes to me sometimes when I stand by the bedside in my emergency department, and look over the ancient form that lies before me, barely aware of anything.

Usually the feeling comes in those times when I am weary and frustrated from making too many decisions too fast, in the middle of the night. Into the midst of this comes a patient from a local nursing home, sent for reasons I can seldom discern.

I walk into the room and sometimes roll my cynical eyes at the nurse. She hands me the minimal data sent with the patient, and I begin the detective work. And just when I'm most annoyed, just when I want to do nothing and send them back, I look at them. And then I touch them. And then, as I imagine my sons, tears well up and I see the error of my thoughts.

For one day, it may be. One day, my little boys, still young enough to kiss me and think me heroic, may lie before another cynical doctor, in the middle of the night of their dementia, and need care. More than medicine, they will need compassion. They will need someone to have the insight to look at them, and say, "Here was once a child, cherished and loved, who played games in the nursery with his mother and father. Here was a child who put teeth under pillows, and loved bedtime stories, crayons and stuffed animals. Here was a treasure of love to a man and a woman long gone. How can I honor them? By treating their child with love and gentility; and by seeing that their child has come full circle to infancy once more, and will soon be born once more into forever.

This vision is frightful because I will not be there to comfort them, or to say, "I am here" when they call out, unless God grants me the gift of speaking across forever. It is painful because I will not be there to serve them as I did in life and see that they are treated as what they are: unique and wonderful, made in the image of the Creator, and of their mother and me. It is terrible because our society treats the aged as worse than a burden; it treats them as tragedies of time. It seems hopeless because when they contract and lie motionless, no one will touch them with the love I have for them, or know the history of their scars, visible and invisible. I am the walking library of their lives, and I will be unavailable. All I can do is ask, while I live, for God's mercy on them as they grow older.

And yet, the image has beauty and hope as well. Because if I see my little boys as aged and infirm, I can dream that their lives were long and rich. I can dream that they filled their lucid years with greatness and love, that they knew God and served Him well, and were men of honor and gentility. I can imagine that even if they live in their shadowland alone, somewhere children and grandchildren, even great-grandchildren thrive. I can hope that their heirs come to see them, and care, and harass the staff of the nursing home to treat Grandpa better. I can hope that they care enough not to allow my boys to suffer, but that they hold no illusions about physical immortality, and will let them come to their mother and me when the time arrives. And best, I can know that their age and illness will only bring the day of that reunion closer.

My career as an emergency physician has taught me something very important about dealing with the sick and injured, whether young or old. It has taught me that the

Golden Rule also can be stated this way: "Do unto others as you would have others do unto your children." I think that this is a powerful way to improve our interactions with others, not just in medicine but in every action of our lives. And it is certainly a unique way to view our treatment of the elderly. For one day all our children will be old. And only if this lesson has been applied will they be treated with anything approaching the love that only we, their parents, hope for them to always have.

Dr. Edwin Leap

Together We Can Make It

After Benjamin Franklin had received a letter thanking him for having done a kindness, he replied: *"As to the kindness you mention, I wish I could have been of more service to you than I have been, but if I had, the only thank you that I should desire is that you would always be ready to serve any other person that may be in need of your assistance in any way; and so let good deeds go around, for mankind are all a family. As for my part, when I am employed in serving others, I do not look upon myself as conferring favors but as paying debts."*

Bob Butler lost his legs in a 1965 land mine explosion in Vietnam. He returned home a war hero. Twenty years later, he proved once again that heroism comes from the heart.

Butler was working in his garage in a small town in Arizona on a hot summer day when he heard a woman's screams coming from a nearby house. He rolled his wheelchair toward the house, but the dense shrubbery wouldn't allow him access to the back door. So the veteran got out of his chair and crawled through the dirt and bushes.

"I had to get there," he says. "It didn't matter how much it hurt."

When Butler arrived at the house, he traced the screams to the pool where a three-year-old girl was lying at the bottom. She had been born without arms and had fallen in the water and couldn't swim. Her mother, who also couldn't swim, stood over her baby screaming frantically. Butler dove to the bottom of the pool and brought little Stephanie up to the deck. Her face was blue, she had no pulse and she was not breathing.

Butler immediately went to work performing CPR to revive her while Stephanie's mother telephoned the fire department. She was told the paramedics were already out on a call. Helplessly, she sobbed and hugged Butler's shoulder.

As Butler continued with his CPR, he calmly reassured Stephanie's mother. "Don't worry," he said. "I was her arms to get out of the pool. It'll be okay. I'm now her lungs. Together we can make it."

Seconds later the little girl coughed, regained consciousness and began to cry. As they hugged and rejoiced together, the mother asked Butler how he knew it would be okay.

"When my legs were blown off in the war, I was all alone in a field," he told her. "No one was there to help except a Vietnamese girl who heard me cry out. As she struggled to drag me into her village, she whispered in broken English, "It okay. It okay. You can live. I be your legs. Together we make it.""

"This was my chance," he told Stephanie's mom, "to return the favor."

Dan Clark

Love is the Crowning Glory

Not what we gain but what we give, measures the worth of the life we live.

Anonymous

The world knows her as "The Queen of the Catwalk," supermodel Sharon "Magic" Jordan whose striking beauty turns heads wherever she goes. She turned my head in Chicago where I met her.

There, she shared with me what she had learned of life, particularly what she had learned about there being another kind of beauty – the beauty of the soul.

Sharon learned of this inner beauty at the knee of her mother and grandmother, where, as a young child, she heard about "doing unto others." It was a lesson she would learn well. For her, kindness became a way of life.

Then in 1978, Sharon was to experience what it felt like to have the floodgates of past kindnesses she had rendered onto others now rendered onto her.

Her dreams had gone up in smoke – literally. A fired raged through her home destroying all that she owned – including the evening gown, swimsuit, shoes and other items she was to wear as a contestant in the Atlanta, Georgia beauty pageant scheduled for the following Saturday night. What was she to do?

Well, word got around, and as it turned out, it would be

others who would do for Sharon what she was unable to do for herself.

Imagine her surprise when one of her friends paid for a room at the Hilton Hotel for her to stay. Imagine her surprise when one of her friends arranged to provide lodging in their own home for Sharon's family who had loaded up their van and come from Florida to help her in any way they could. Imagine her surprise when one of her friends knew a friend of a friend who could sew a designer gown, replacing the one she had lost. And imagine her surprise when one of her friends came through with a swimming suit and shoes.

But mostly, imagine Sharon's surprise when she was crowned the following Saturday night on that runway as the winner. It was a moment that truly ended up launching her career.

And just one question remained: Was it her physical beauty – or the beauty of her soul – that ultimately put Sharon under the spotlight?

And Sharon knew the answer.

He who wishes to secure the good of others has already secured his own.

Confucius

Chapter 2 – Summary

Charitable Giving, Charitable Living

Every kindness spreads in a shining circle. See how good people everywhere set rings of light moving across the darkness, rings that link and interlock and keep at bay the forces of the night.

Pam Brown

Kindness. Generosity. Love. These are Life's spiritual jewels. They are the virtues of goodness and light. Each brings its blessings to our days and makes life worth the living when we choose to participate in them.

In the preceding stories and quotations shared, one common conclusion can be made: When we bring love into the lives of those around us, we bring love into our own life. Love circles back to bless its bestower, and becomes its own reward. We create love by being loving. And thus, we ourselves give life to love, or we ourselves deny it existence.

What would our world be like without love? Without generosity? Without kindness?

It's not as difficult of a question to answer as one would first suppose. To imagine a world void of these virtues, one needs to look no further than to individual lives that are void of them and to the persons living those lives who believe they have been abandoned by Love.

It is tempting to believe that it is possible for Love to abandon us - especially when the darkness of our life is at a premium and light seems nowhere to be found. However, as the stories shared illustrate, a world without love, or a life without love, can only be created by those who choose not to participate in love. The more we participate in loving acts and in kindly deeds, the more evidence of love fills our lives.

Love does not abandon us – not ever. It does not, because it cannot. Only we can abandon *it*. Every moment of every minute, of every hour, of every day, we have access to Love's power and to the depth, meaning and value it can bestow upon our lives. It exists eternally, and springs from the same Life Force we were created as an extension of.

Do you desire to make Love your priority? Are you ready to commit to living a more loving life? Then begin by determining to do so. This does not mean you will need to make radical changes overnight to your lifestyle, but rather, what it does mean is that you are ready to begin to make little changes that will yield big differences in the spiritual quality of your life. As you participate in serving others around you with small kindnesses, and then build upon those kindnesses with even more simple acts of generosity and love, your charitable giving will begin to turn into charitable living, a way of life encompassing both financial generosity to the needy among us, as well as spiritual generosity to those in need of our prayers, time, and encouragement.

Get started by doing a little something each day in terms of thoughtfulness to others. This can be as simple as complimenting a stranger on her hairstyle or it can be something that involves more thought like surprising the fellow in the toll booth you pass through every morning with a cup of hot chocolate from the gas station down the road or sending your child's teacher a note that says, "I appreciate you."

Or maybe you might consider becoming a Big Brother to a troubled teen or volunteering at your local library to deliver books to shut-ins on Tuesday evenings. Libraries, hospitals, museums, homeless shelters and nursing homes are just a few of the organizations in need of volunteers on a regular basis. Consider contacting your local volunteer center to learn more about the "how's" of volunteering and also to find out specific options available to you in your own community to begin investing your time for the benefit of others.

Whether your efforts to live lovingly are structured and scheduled, or spontaneous and spur-of-the-moment, it is important to remember that there is no right or wrong way to go about things. There is as much value in becoming a Girl Scout Leader as there is in delivering a homemade casserole and a loaf of banana nut bread to your neighbor who was just released from the hospital. There is as much value in organizing a community food drive as there is in praying for your loved ones while you fold laundry or do the dishes.

In the beginning, you may find it helpful to journal your kindnesses until your commitment to live lovingly becomes a way of life. A journal can be a useful tool in keeping you disciplined and accountable. You may also want to write your favorite inspirational quotations that motivate you toward kindness throughout the pages. One of my personal favorites is by Charles Kingsley and reads, "Make a rule and pray to God to help you keep it, never, if possible, to lie down at night without being able to say, 'I have made one human being a little wiser, or a little happier, or at least a little better this day."

Finally, remember to reflect regularly and often on how your life is bearing witness to your commitment. This is very important, for ultimately, it is not what we say, but what we do, which evidences our priorities.

As an example, I ask you this: Can we really say spending quality time together as a family is a priority to us if we do not regularly participate in quality time together as a family? Just so, can we really say "living lovingly is a priority to me" if our life does not evidence this?

To determine what your priorities are – what matters most to you – take a close look at the activities that fill your days. These are your priorities.

Is love among them?

If not, it can be. Each of us can commit ourselves to the great privilege of blessing those among us who are in need of a little happiness or a little betterment. When we take time – and make time - to consistently give place to love, we begin to see with the eyes of our heart that love, love alone, is the most valuable use of our life. Tapping into love is tapping into the mother lode of our spirit. It is hitting the spiritual vein of gold that gives our hearts access to the treasures of joy, peace, and happiness. It is then, when our hearts begin to brim full of the wealth that only loving can bring us, we discover we are becoming rich in all that really matters in the end.

CHAPTER 3

Turning From Anger to Forgiveness

Raising the Bar

Teach me to feel another's woe,
To hide the fault I see;
That mercy I to others show,
That mercy shows to me.

Alexander Pope

Love. How would you define it?

In order to live lovingly, one must first determine what love is. This belief then becomes the guide we live our lives by and the focal point for our choices to be processed against.

So, what is love?

Perhaps the most familiar attempt to capture in words what love means comes to us from Saint Paul who wrote: *Love is patient, love is kind. Love does not envy, love does not boast, love is not proud. Love is not rude, love is not self-seeking, love is not easily angered, love keeps no record of wrongs.*

These words provided a spiritual compass for Paul's life, and they can provide the same direction to ours. Do you seek to live in the realm of love? Is love the goal of your heart? Do you wish to understand love's meaning on a deeper level in order to apply it more fully to your life?

If so, try this: re-read Paul's words above and personalize them by replacing every word "love" with your own name. Pay close attention as you read to the progression of

Paul's definition. It becomes evident as one does so that Paul is raising the bar on what it is that love expects of us as he furthers his thoughts. He begins with actions – patience and kindness – and moves into attitudes – envy, boastfulness, rudeness, pride. Then he cranks it up and tells us that love is not self-seeking, essentially tells us that we are living lovingly when our lives become more about others than about ourselves.

Then the bar goes up from there to a higher love, a love that is not easily angered, a love that keeps no record of wrongs.

It is this love we find at the cross in the words spoken by the One nailed there, praying, "Father, forgive them; for they know not what they do."

It is this same love we find in the Hindu leader Gandhi, dying in the dust at the feet of the assassin who fired three bullets into him – three bullets at close range. In these last moments of his life, the great leader moved his hand to his forehead and made a simple Hindu gesture. Its meaning? "I forgive you." Love spoke silently, but speak it did.

Paul understood the meaning of love and he understood its importance. Writing in the New Testament, he compared love against faith and he compared love against hope. Then he offered his opinion as to which of these three he believed to be the greatest. It was love. "And now these three remain: faith, hope and love," wrote Paul, "but the greatest of these is love." Paul's words are clear: love is greatest. Greater than hope, even greater than faith. No one needs a theology degree to understand Paul's words. Misunderstanding his message would be like misunderstanding "the grass is green" or "the sky is blue." Love is greatest of all.

Let us seek love as the goal of our hearts. Let us begin to raise the bar on our lives. One inch to two inches, two inches to three, then upward, together.

"Press on," urged Paul. "Persevere, be diligent, aim for perfection, never tire, strive, engage in strict training, give yourself wholly, let your progress be seen by all." Saint Paul's writings, as recorded in the Bible, read like a track and field manual in spiritual fitness. Using language of determination and discipline, Paul spiritually lays out the "how to's" for developing a loving life. From kindness to compassion, from gentleness to generosity, he takes us higher and higher.

Then he challenges our souls higher still toward mercy, grace and forgiveness. "Make every effort to do what leads to peace," wrote Paul. "Get rid of all bitterness, rage and anger, brawling and slander, along with every form of malice. Don't grumble against each other. Do not let any unwholesome talk come out of your mouths, but only what is helpful for building others up. Forgive each other. Do not repay anyone evil for evil. Do not take revenge. When cursed, bless. When slandered, answer kindly. If someone is caught in a sin, you who are spiritual should restore him gently. Bear with the failings of the weak."

This is the higher love. Let us seek it as the goal of our hearts – this love that is canyon deep and ocean wide – and let us raise the bar on our lives. One inch to two inches, two inches to three, then onward and upward, together.

The entire law is summed up in a single command: "Love your neighbor as yourself."

If you keep on biting and devouring each other, watch out or you will be destroyed by each other.

Galatians 5:14-15

The Bible

The grudge you hold onto is like a hot coal that you intend to throw at someone, but you're the one who gets burned.

Buddha

Dear Abby:

A young man from a wealthy family was about to graduate from high school. It was the custom in that affluent neighborhood for the parents to give the graduate an automobile. Bill and his father had spent months looking at vehicles, and the week before graduation they found the perfect car. Bill was certain that the car would be his on graduation night.

Imagine his disappointment when, on the eve of his graduation, Bill's father handed him a gift-wrapped Bible! Bill was so angry, he threw the Bible down and stormed out of the house. He and his father never saw each other again. It was the news of his father's death that brought Bill home again.

As he sat one night, going through his father's possessions that he was to inherit, he came across the Bible his father had given him. He brushed away the dust and opened it to find a cashier's check, dated the day of his graduation, in the exact amount of the car they had chosen together.

Beckah Fink

Life is an Empty Bottle

Anger is a destructive emotion which distorts the mind. It is a useless waste of energy for in hurting someone else, you have accomplished nothing except to hurt yourself. This wasteful emotion devours you.

Dr. Maxwell Maltz

Earlier this century, a woman went to her doctor with a catalogue of complaints about her health. The physician examined her thoroughly and became convinced that there was nothing physically wrong with her. He suspected it was her negative outlook on life - her bitterness and resentment - that was the key to her feeling the way she did.

The wise physician took the woman into a back room in his office where he kept some of his medicine. He showed her a shelf filled with empty bottles.

He said to her: "See those bottles? Notice that they are all empty. They are shaped differently from one another, but basically they are all alike.

"Most importantly, they have nothing in them. Now, I can take one of these bottles and fill it with poison - enough poison to kill a human being. Or I can fill it with enough medicine to bring down a fever, or ease a throbbing headache, or fight bacteria in one part of the body. The important thing is that I make the choice. I can fill it with whatever I choose."

The doctor looked her in the eye and said, "Each day

that we are given is basically like one of these empty bottles. We can choose to fill it with love and life-affirming thoughts and attitudes, or we can fill it with destructive, poisonous thoughts. The choice is ours."

And what will we choose? Life-affirming, positive, healing thoughts? Or the seething poisons of anger and bitterness? The choice is ours.

As cited in *Sower's Seeds Aplenty*
by Brian Cavanaugh

If I have learned anything in life it is that bitterness consumes the vessel that contains it.

Rubin Hurricane Carter

The Law of Life

Whatever you give away today
Or think or say or do,
Will multiply about tenfold
And then return to you.

It may not come immediately
Nor from the obvious source,
But The Law applies unfailingly
Through some invisible force.

Whatever you feel about another
Be it love or angered passion,
Will surely bounce right back to you
In some clear or secret fashion.

If you speak about some person
A word of praise or two,
Soon tens of other people
Will speak kind words to you.

Our thoughts are broadcasts of the soul,
Not secrets of the brain;
Kind ones bring us happiness,
Petty ones, untold pain.

Giving works as surely as
Reflection in a mirror,
If hate you send, hate you'll get back,
But loving brings love nearer.

Remember as you start this day
And duty crowds your mind,
That kindness comes so quickly back
To those who first are kind.

Let that thought and this one
Direct you through each day:
The only things we ever keep
Are the things we give away.

                                    Jerry Buchanan

Loving Your Enemies

I believe that the first test of a truly great man is his humility. I don't mean by humility, doubt of his power. But really great men have a curious feeling that the greatness is not of them, but through them. And they see something Divine in every other man and are endlessly, incredibly merciful.

John Ruskin

Abraham Lincoln left for all history a magnificent drama of reconciliation.

When he was campaigning for the presidency, one of his arch-enemies was a man named Edwin Stanton. For some reason Stanton hated Lincoln. He used every ounce of his energy to degrade Lincoln in the eyes of the public. So deep-rooted was Stanton's hate for Lincoln that he uttered unkind words about his physical appearance and sought to embarrass him at every point with the bitterest diatribes. But in spite of this, Lincoln was elected the sixteenth President of the United States.

Then came the period when Lincoln had to select his cabinet which would consist of the persons who would be his most intimate associates in implementing his programs. He started choosing men here and there for the various positions.

The day finally came for Lincoln to select the all-impor-

162

tant post of the Secretary of War. Can you imagine whom Lincoln chose to fill this post? None other than the man named Stanton.

There was an immediate uproar in the President's inner circle when the news began to spread. Advisor after advisor was heard saying, "Mr. President, you are making a mistake. Do you know this man Stanton? Are you familiar with all the ugly things he said about you? He is your enemy. He will seek to sabotage your programs. Have you thought this through, Mr. President?"

Mr. Lincoln's answer was to the point: "Yes, I know Mr. Stanton. I am aware of all the terrible things he has said about me. But after looking over the nation, I find he is the best man for the job." So Stanton became Abraham Lincoln's Secretary of War and rendered an invaluable service to his nation and to his President.

Not many years later Lincoln was assassinated. Many laudable things were said about him. But of all the great statements made about Abraham Lincoln, the words of Stanton remain among the greatest. Standing near the dead body of the man he once hated, Stanton referred to him as one of the greatest men who ever lived, saying, "There lies the most perfect ruler of men the world has ever seen and now he belongs to the ages."

As cited in *Sower's Seeds of Virtue*
by Brian Cavanaugh

Unto Thee I Grant:
The Understanding of Anger

Anger is an acid which does more harm to the vessel in which it is stored than to the object on which it is poured.
Anonymous

As the whirlwind in its fury teareth up trees, and deformeth the face of nature, or as an earthquake in its convulsions overturneth whole cities; so the rage of an angry man throweth mischief around him. Danger and destruction wait on his hand.

But consider, and forget not thine own weakness; so thou may pardon the failings of others.

Indulge not thyself in the passion of anger; it is whetting a sword to wound thine own breast... If thou bearest slight provocations with patience, it shall be imputed unto thee for wisdom; and if thou wipest them from thy remembrance, thy heart shall not reproach thee.

Seeth thou not that the angry man loseth his understanding? Whilst thou art yet in thy senses, let the wrath of another be a lesson to thyself.

Do nothing in a passion. Why wilt thou put to sea in the violence of a storm?

If it be difficult to rule thine anger, it is wise to prevent it; avoid therefore all occasions of falling into wrath, or guard thyself against them whenever they occur.

Harbor not revenge in thy breast; it will torment thy heart...be always more ready to forgive, than to return an injury; he that watches for an opportunity of revenge, lieth in wait against himself, and draweth down mischief on his own head.

A mild answer to an angry man, like water cast upon the fire, abateth his heat; and from an enemy he shall become thy friend.

Tibetan Wisdom

"I am sorry for him; I couldn't be angry with my uncle if I tried. Who suffers by his ill whims? Himself always."

Scrooge's Nephew, Fred
A Christmas Carol
by Charles Dickens

Good Will, Ill Will

Resentment is like taking poison and waiting for the other person to die.

Malachy McCourt

When Terry Anderson, a correspondent for *The Associated Press*, was released by his Lebanese captors, he looked surprisingly vigorous and healthy. Despite nearly seven years of deprivation, hardship, physical and emotional punishment, he managed to survive his ordeal successfully.

Anderson described to reporters the agony of his life in chains and blindfolds, food flung on the floor, and a life of rigid rules enforced by brutal guards.

"I was desperate to keep my brain alive," he stated to the press. "I was deadly scared that I would lapse into some kind of mental rot. What kept me going was my faith and my stubbornness. You wake up every day and summon up the energy."

I believe with all my heart that there is a power that can give us good health of body, mind, and soul. But our thinking must be right, and many need to deal with their negative and destructive thoughts. Never forget Who created you. And never forget Who can constantly re-create you.

Many people are sick in their thoughts. Take resentment, for example. The word *resentment* comes from a basic root word meaning to re-hurt. Suppose you do something to me, and I resent it. Then I go home and I tell my wife, "Bill Jones did this to me."

The first experience hurt me when Bill Jones did it. I re-hurt myself when I mentioned it to my wife. So the next day I say to her, "I'm sure going to get even with Bill Jones for that mean thing he did to me." So I've hurt myself three times now. And I haven't yet hurt Bill Jones once!

The next day, I say to someone else, "That Bill Jones is a mean character. You know what he did to me?" So I've re-hurt myself four times. And, if I keep on doing this, I create a festering sore inside myself. I become sick in my mind and soul, and ultimately become sick in my body.

To resent, is to have ill will toward another. Do you know why they call it ill will? Because it is sick will. It is amazing what these ill thoughts will do to you. But when you have good will, you have healthy will.

Norman Vincent Peale

Anger's Poisonous Bite

The longer we dwell on our misfortunes, the greater their power to harm us.

Anonymous

A trapped rattlesnake can become so angry it will bite itself.

That's a good image of what happens when we let anger control us. We end up biting ourselves, not our enemy. We end up destroying ourselves more than we destroy our enemy.

More and more doctors are becoming increasingly aware that at the root of many illnesses is unresolved anger. Until the ill person learns to deal with this anger, no medicine can help.

Mark Link

Love Your Enemy

To forgive is the highest, most beautiful form of love.
In return, you will receive untold peace and happiness.

Robert Muller

It was in a church in Munich that I saw him - a balding, heavyset man in a gray overcoat, a brown felt hat clutched between his hands. People were filing out of the basement room where I had just spoken, moving along the rows of wooden chairs to the door at the rear. It was 1947 and I had come from Holland to defeated Germany with the message that God forgives.

It was the truth they needed most to hear in that bitter, bombed-out land, and I gave them my favorite mental picture. Maybe because the sea is never far from a Hollander's mind, I liked to think of the Bible verse that says our forgiven sins are thrown to the bottom of the sea.

"When we confess our sins," I said, "God casts them into the deepest ocean, gone forever. God then places a sign out there that says, 'NO FISHING ALLOWED.'"

The solemn faces stared back at me, not quite daring to believe. There were never questions after a talk in Germany in 1947. People stood up in silence, in silence collected their coats, in silence left the room.

And that's when I saw him, working his way forward against the others. One moment I saw the overcoat and the brown hat; the next, my memory flashed back to see him wearing a blue uniform and a visored cap with its skull and cross bones. It came back with a rush: the huge room with its harsh overhead lights; the pathetic pile of dresses and shoes in the center of the floor; the shame of walking naked past *this* man. I could see my sister's frail form ahead of me, ribs sharp beneath the parchment skin. *Betsie, how thin you were!*

My memory was of the place called Ravensbruck, a concentration camp where I had been imprisoned, and the man who was making his way forward now had been a guard there - one of the most cruel guards.

Now he was in front of me, hand thrust out: "A fine message, *Fraulein*! How good it is to know that, as you say, all our sins are at the bottom of the sea!"

And I, who had spoken so glibly of forgiveness only moments ago, fumbled in my pocketbook rather than take *that* hand. He would not remember me, of course - how could he remember one prisoner among those thousands of women?

But I remembered him and the leather crop swinging from his belt. I was now face-to-face with one of my captors and my blood seemed to freeze.

"You mentioned Ravensbruck in your talk," he was saying. "I was a guard there." (No, he did not remember me.) "But since that time," he went on, "I have become a Christian. I know that God has forgiven me for the cruel things I did there, but I would like to hear it from your lips as well. *Fraulein*" - again the hand came out - "will you forgive me?"

And I stood there - I, whose sins had again and again needed to be forgiven - could not forgive him. My sister Betsie had died in that place. Could he erase her slow terrible death simply for the asking?

It could not have been many seconds that he stood there - hand held out - but to me it seemed hours as I wrestled with the most difficult thing I had ever had to do.

For I had to do it. I knew that. The message that God forgives has a prior condition: that we forgive those who have injured us. "If you do not forgive men their trespasses," Jesus says, "neither will your Father in Heaven forgive your trespasses." I knew it not only as a commandment of God, but as a daily experience. Since the end of the war I had had a home in Holland for victims of Nazi brutality. Those who were able to forgive their former enemies were able also to return to the outside world and rebuild their lives, no matter what the physical scars. Those who nursed their bitterness remained invalids. It was as simple and horrible as that.

And still I stood there with the coldness clutching my heart. But forgiveness is not an emotion - I knew that too. Forgiveness is an act of the will, and the will can function regardless of the temperature of the heart. *Jesus, please help me!* I prayed silently. *I can lift my hand, I can do that much. You supply the feeling.*

And so woodenly, mechanically, I thrust my hand into the one stretched out to me. And as I did, an incredible thing took place. The current started in my shoulder, raced down my arm and sprang into our joined hands. And then this healing warmth seemed to flood my whole being, bringing tears to my eyes.

"I forgive you, brother!" I cried. "With all my heart, I forgive you!"

For a long moment we grasped each other's hands - the former guard and the former prisoner. I had never known God's love so intensely as I did then. But even so, I realized it was not my love. I had tried, and did not have the power. It was the power God.

Corrie ten Boom

Setting others free means setting yourself free, because resentment is really a form of attachment. It is a Cosmic Truth that it takes two to make a prisoner; the prisoner and the jailer. When you hold resentment against anyone, you are bound to that person by a cosmic link, a real, though mental chain. You are tied by a cosmic tie to the thing you hate.

Emmet Fox

Love is Vital

I have learned that love, not time, heals all wounds.

Andy Rooney

The need to love and to be loved is paramount. It is the magic of love that keeps our spirits alive and sustains our hearts and souls. And as "the heartbeat of the universe," love is the single most important force shaping our physical, emotional, and spiritual lives.

To this point, a man recalls what a seasoned physician once said to him: "I have been practicing medicine for thirty years, and I have prescribed many things. But in the long run I have learned that for most of what ails the human creature the best medicine is love."

"What if it doesn't work?" the man asked, to which the physician replied, "Double the dose."

Jo Ann Larsen

What is the Meaning of Life?

C.S. Lewis wrote, "Everyone says forgiveness is a lovely idea until they have something to forgive..." Unfortunately, when we need its healing power most, forgiveness may seem neither a lovely idea nor an empowering one - only elusive, at best. And so, victimized once by whatever wrongs were done to us, we victimize ourselves again and again by allowing anger to take up residence in and drain vitality from our souls. Life is a wonderful gift to be treasured and shared. But anger and resentment, fed by a refusal to forgive, block healing and growth. The gift becomes damaged - and all of us lose.

David W. Schell

"Are there any questions?" An offer that comes at the end of college lectures and long meetings. Said when an audience is not only overdosed with information, but when there is no time left anyhow. At times like that you sure do have questions. Like, "Can we leave now?" and "What the heck was this meeting for?" and "Where can I get a drink?"

The gesture is suppose to indicate openness on the part of the speaker, I suppose, but if in fact you do ask a question, both the speaker and the audience will give you drop-dead looks. And some fool - some earnest idiot - always asks. And the speaker always answers by repeating most of what he has already said.

But if there is a little time left and there is a little silence in response to the invitation, I usually ask the most important question of all: "What is the meaning of life?" You never know, somebody may have the answer, and I'd really hate to miss it because I was too socially inhibited to ask. But when I ask, it's usually taken as a kind of absurdist move - people laugh and nod and gather up their stuff and the meeting is dismissed on that ridiculous note.

Once, and only once, I asked that question and got a serious answer. One that is with me still. First, I must tell you where this happened, because the place has a power of its own. In Greece, near the village of Gonia, on a rocky bay off the island of Crete, sits a Greek Orthodox monastery. Alongside it, on land donated by the monastery, is an institute dedicated to human understanding and peace, and especially to rapprochement between Germans and Cretans, an improbable task, given the bitter residue of wartime.

This site is important, because it overlooks the small airstrip at Maleme where Nazi paratroopers invaded Crete and were attacked by peasants wielding kitchen knives and hay scythes. The retribution was terrible. The populations of whole villages were lined up and shot for assaulting Hitler's finest troops. High above the institute is a cemetery with a single cross marking the mass grave of Cretan partisans. And across the bay on yet another hill is the regimented burial ground of the Nazi paratroopers. The memorials are so placed that all might see and never forget. Hate was the only weapon the Cretans had at the end, and it was a weapon many vowed never to give up. Never ever.

Against this heavy curtain of history, in this place where the stone of hatred is hard and thick, the existence of an institute devoted to healing the wounds of war is a fragile paradox. How has it come to be here? The answer is a man. Alexander Papaderos, a doctor of philosophy, teacher, politician, resident of Athens but a son of this soil. At war's end he came to believe that the Germans and the Cretans had much to give one another - much to learn from one another; that they had an example to set. For if they could forgive each other and construct a creative relationship, then any people could.

To make a lovely story short, Papaderos succeeded. The institute became a reality - a conference ground on the site of horror - and it was in fact a source of productive interaction between the two countries. Books have been written on the dreams that were realized by what people gave to people in this place.

By the time I came to the institute for a summer session, Alexander Papaderos had become a living legend. One look at him and you saw his strength and intensity - energy, physical power, courage, intelligence, passion, and vivacity radiated from his person. And to speak to him, to shake his hand, to be in a room with him when he spoke, was to experience his extraordinary electric humanity. Few men live up to their reputations when you get close. Alexander Papaderos was an exception.

At the last session on the last morning of a two-week seminar on Greek culture, led by intellectuals and experts in their fields who were recruited by Papaderos from across

Greece, Papaderos rose from his chair at the back of the room and walked to the front, where he stood in the bright Greek sunlight of an open window and looked out. We followed his gaze across the bay to the iron cross marking the German cemetery.

He turned and made the ritual gesture: "Are there any questions?"

Quiet quilted the room. These two weeks had generated enough questions for a lifetime, but for now there was only silence.

"No questions?" Papaderos swept the room with his eyes.

So, I asked.

"Dr. Papaderos, what is the meaning of life?"

The usual laughter followed, and people stirred to go. Papaderos held up his hand and stilled the room and looked at me for a long time, asking with his eyes if I was serious and seeing from my eyes that I was.

"I will answer your question," he said, and then taking his wallet out of his hip pocket, he fished into a leather billfold and brought out a very small round mirror, about the size of a quarter.

What he said went like this:

"When I was a small child, during the war, we were very poor and we lived in a remote village. One day, on the road, I found the broken pieces of a mirror. A German motorcycle had been wrecked in that place. I tried to find all the pieces and put them together, but it was not possible, so I kept only the largest piece. This one. And by scratching it on a stone I made it round. I began to play with it as a toy and became fascinated by the fact that I could reflect light into dark places where the sun would never shine - in deep holes and crevices and dark closets. It became a game for me to get light into the most inaccessible places I could find.

"I kept the little mirror, and as I went about my growing up, I would take it out in idle moments and continue the challenge of the game. As I became a man, I grew to understand that this was not just a child's game but a metaphor for what I might do with my life. I came to understand that I am not the light or the source of light. But light - truth, understanding, knowledge - is there, and it will only shine in many dark places if I reflect it.

"I am a fragment of a mirror whose whole design and shape I do not know. Nevertheless, with what I have I can reflect light into the dark places of this world - into the black places in the hearts of men - and change some things in some people. Perhaps others may see and do likewise. This is what I am about. This is the meaning of my life."

And then he took his small mirror and, holding it carefully, caught the bright rays of daylight streaming through the window and reflected them onto my face and onto my hands folded on the desk.

Much of what I experienced in the way of information about Greek culture and history that summer is gone from my memory. But in the wallet of my mind I carry a small round mirror still.

Robert Fulghum

Prayer of Peace

Blessed are the peacemakers...
Matthew 5:9

Lord, make me an instrument of your peace.
Where there is hatred let me sow love,
Where there is injury let me sow forgiveness,
Where there is discord let me sow harmony,
Where there is doubt, faith,
Where there is despair, hope,
Where there is darkness, light,
Where there is sadness, joy.
Lord, grant that I may seek rather to comfort than
to be comforted,
To understand than to be understood,
To love than to be loved.
For it is by giving that one receives,
It is by forgetting self that one finds,
It is in forgiving that one is forgiven,
And it is in dying that we are born to eternal life.
Saint Francis of Assisi

Carl's Garden

*There is no difficulty that enough love will not con-
quer. It makes no difference how deeply seated may be the
trouble, how hopeless the outlook, how muddled the tangle,
how great the mistake. A sufficient realization of love will
dissolve it all.*

Emmet Fox

Carl was a quiet man. He didn't talk much. He would
always greet you with a big smile and a firm handshake.
Even after living in our neighborhood for over 50 years, no
one could really say they knew him very well.

Before his retirement, he took the bus to work each
morning. The lone sight of him walking down the street
often worried us. He had a slight limp from a bullet wound
received during the war. Watching him, we worried that
although he had survived the war, he may not make it
through our changing uptown neighborhood with its ever-
increasing random violence, gangs, and drug activity.

When he saw the flyer at our local church asking for volunteers to care for the gardens behind the minister's residence, he responded in his characteristically unassuming
manner. Without fanfare, he just signed up.

He was well into his 87th year when the very thing we
had always feared finally happened.

He was just finishing his watering for the day when

182

three gang members approached him. Ignoring their attempt to intimidate him, he simply asked, "Would you like a drink from the hose?"

The tallest and toughest-looking of the three said, "Yeah, sure," with a malevolent little smile. As Carl offered the hose to him, the other two grabbed Carl's arm, throwing him down. As the hose snaked crazily over the ground, dousing everything in its way, Carl's assailants stole his retirement watch and his wallet, and then fled. Carl tried to get himself up, but he had been thrown down on his bad leg.

He lay there trying to gather himself as the minister came running to help him. Although the minister witnessed the attack from his window, he couldn't get there fast enough to stop it.

"Carl, are you okay? Are you hurt?" the minister kept asking as he helped Carl to his feet. Carl just passed a hand over his brow and sighed, shaking his head.

"Just some kids. I hope they'll wise-up someday." His wet clothes clung to his slight frame as he bent to pick up the hose. He adjusted the nozzle again and started to water.

Confused and a little concerned, the minister asked, "Carl, what are you doing?"

"I've got to finish my watering. It's been very dry lately," came the calm reply. Satisfying himself that Carl really was all right, the minister could only marvel. Carl was a man from a different time and place.

A few weeks later the three returned. Just as before their threat was unchallenged. Carl again offered them a drink from his hose.

This time they didn't rob him. They wrenched the hose from his hand and drenched him head to foot in the icy water. When they had finished their humiliation of him, they sauntered off down the street, yelling curses, falling over one another laughing at the hilarity of what they had just done.

Carl just watched them. Then he turned toward the warmth giving sun, picked up the hose, and went on with his watering.

The summer was quickly fading into fall. Carl was doing some tilling when he was startled by the sudden approach of someone behind him. He stumbled and fell into some evergreen branches. As he struggled to regain his footing, he turned to see the tall leader of his summer tormenters reaching down for him. He braced himself for the expected attack. "Don't worry old man, I'm not gonna hurt you this time." The young man spoke softly, still offering the tattooed and scarred hand to Carl. As he helped Carl get up, the man pulled a crumpled bag from his pocket and handed it to Carl.

"What's this?" Carl asked.

"It's your stuff," the young man explained. "It's your stuff back. Even the money in your wallet."

"I don't understand," Carl said. "Why would you help me now?"

The man shifted his feet, seeming embarrassed and ill at ease. "I learned something from you," he said. "I ran with that gang and hurt people like you. We picked you because you were old and we knew we could do it. But every time we came and did something to you, instead of yelling and fighting back, you tried to give us a drink. You didn't hate us for hating you. You kept showing love against our hate." He stopped for a moment. "I couldn't sleep after we stole your stuff, so here it is back."

He paused for another awkward moment, not knowing what more there was to say. "That bag's my way of saying thanks for straightening me out, I guess." And with that he walked off down the street.

Carl looked down at the sack in his hands and gingerly opened it. He took out the retirement watch and put it back on his wrist. Opening his wallet, he checked for his wedding photo. He gazed for a moment at the young bride that still smiled back at him from all those years ago.

He died one cold day after Christmas that winter. Many people attended his funeral in spite of the weather. In particular the minister noticed a tall young man that he didn't know sitting quietly in a distant corner of the church. The minister spoke of Carl's garden as a lesson in life. In a voice made thick with unshed tears, he said, "Do your best and make your garden as beautiful as you can. We will never forget Carl and his garden."

The following spring another flyer went up. It read: "Person needed to care for Carl's garden." The flyer went unnoticed by the busy parishioners until one day a knock was heard at the minister's office door. Opening the door, the minister saw a pair of scarred and tattooed hands holding the flyer. "I believe this is my job, if you'll have me," the young man said.

The minister recognized him as the same young man who had returned the stolen watch and wallet to Carl. He knew that Carl's kindness had turned this man's life around. As the minister handed him the keys to the garden shed, he said, "Yes, go take care of Carl's garden and honor him."

The man went to work and, over the next several years, he tended the flowers and vegetables just as Carl had done. In that time, he went to college, got married, and became a prominent member of the community. But he never forgot his promise to Carl's memory and kept the garden as beautiful as he thought Carl would have kept it.

One day he approached the new minister and told him that he couldn't care for the garden any longer. He explained with a shy and happy smile, "My wife just had a baby boy last night, and she's bringing him home on Saturday."

"Well, congratulations!" said the minister, as he was handed the garden shed keys. "That's wonderful! What's the baby's name?"

"Carl," he replied.

Author Unknown

Love and pity and wish well to every soul in the world; dwell in love, and then you dwell in God; hate nothing but the evil that stirs within your own heart.

William Law

Forgiving an Enemy

The weak can never forgive. Forgiveness is an attribute of the strong.

Mahatmas Gandhi

In 1946 Czeslaw Godlewski was a member of a gang of youths that roamed and sacked the German countryside. On one isolated farm, they gunned down ten members of the Hamelmann family. Nine of them died, but the father, Wilhelm, miraculously survived four bullet wounds.

As the time approached for Godlewski to complete his twenty-year prison term, the state would not release him simply because he had nowhere to go. None of his family members offered shelter, and each place the state sought to place him refused to take him. Then the warden received a letter. It contained a simple request, "I ask you to release Godlewski to my custody and care. Christ died for my sins and forgave me. Should I not then forgive this man?" The letter was signed, Wilhelm Hamelmann.

Lord Balfour once advised, "The best thing to give to your enemy is forgiveness; to an opponent, tolerance." If these are the best we can give to our enemies and opponents, how much more should we grant forgiveness and tolerance to those we love!

God's Little Daily Devotional

What is the Perfect Gift?

To forgive is to permanently shed hurt feelings and to put something away. It means drawing a line under something and saying, 'Finished.' Whatever the horror, whatever the nightmare, it's over because it's forgiven. The courage to forgive is gigantic, and the courage to acknowledge the need to forgive is perhaps even greater.

Edward Crowther

Tick. Tock.

Thanksgiving Day was fast approaching and the biggest shopping day of the year was on its heels. Christmas was coming and everyone would soon be out and about in search of the perfect gift.

And what exactly *is* the perfect gift?

Well, a newspaper columnist posed that exact question to her readers a number of years ago.

When the answers were tallied, the overwhelming top response came as a bit of a surprise since it had nothing to do with price tags or malls.

The perfect gift? Forgiveness.

The House by the Side of the Road

There are hermit souls that live withdrawn
In the place of their self-content;
There are souls like stars, that dwell apart,
In a fellowless firmament;
There are pioneer souls that blaze their paths
Where highways never ran -
But let me live in a house by the side of the road
And be a friend to man.

Let me live in a house by the side of the road,
Where the race of men go by -
The men who are good and the men who are bad,
As good and as bad as I.
I would not sit in the scorner's seat,
Or hurl the cynic's ban -
Let me live in a house by the side of the road
And be a friend to man.

I see from my house by the side of the road,
By the side of the highway of life,
The men who press with the ardor of hope,
The men who are faint with strife.
But I turn not away from their smiles nor their
tears, both parts of an infinite plan -
Let me live in a house by the side of the road
And be a friend to man.

Let me live in my house by the side of the road -
It's here the race of men go by.
They are good, they are bad, they are weak, they
are strong,
Wise, foolish - so am I;
Then why should I sit in the scorner's seat,
Or hurl the cynic's ban?
Let me live in my house by the side of the road
And be a friend to man.

Sam Walter Foss

A Word of Warning

Those at war with others are not at peace with them-selves.

William Hazlitt

"Let not the sun go down upon thy wrath." These famil-iar words, found in the Biblical book of Ephesians, are one of many writings that provide a warning to readers about the emotion of anger.

We are human. We all experience anger. However, as the verse above indicates, we are not to carry this poisonous emotion around with us - from one day into the next - allow-ing it to seed within our heart.

We need to take control of it, before it takes control of us.

Follow peace with all men...lest any root of bitterness springing up trouble you...

Hebrews 12:14-15 KJV

Defining Heaven and Hell

If you don't like what you're getting back in life, take a close look at what you're putting out.

Anonymous

A big, tough samurai once went to see a little monk.

"Monk," he said, in a voice accustomed to instant obedience, "teach me about heaven and hell!"

The monk looked up at this mighty warrior and replied with utter disdain, "Teach you about heaven and hell? I couldn't teach you about anything. You're dirty. You smell. Your blade is rusty. You're a disgrace, an embarrassment to the samurai class. Get out of my sight. I can't stand you."

The samurai was furious. He shook, got all red in the face, and was speechless with rage. He pulled out his sword and raised it above him, preparing to slay the monk.

"That's hell," said the monk softly.

The samurai was overwhelmed. The compassion and surrender of this little man who had offered his life to give this teaching to show him hell! He slowly put down his sword, filled with gratitude and suddenly peaceful.

"And that's heaven," said the monk softly.

Jack Kornfield
& Christina Feldman

Paco Come Home

Forgiveness is as valuable to the one forgiven as to the one who forgives.

Amish Proverb

In a small town in Spain, a man named Jorge had a bitter argument with his young son Paco. The next day Jorge discovered that Paco's bed was empty - he had run away from home.

Overcome with remorse, Jorge searched his soul and realized that his son was more important to him than anything else. He wanted to start over. Jorge went to a well-known store in the center of town and posted a large sign that read, "Paco, come home. I love you. Meet me here tomorrow morning." It was signed: Your Father.

The next morning Jorge went to the store where he found seven young boys named Paco who had also run away from home. They were all answering the call of love, hoping it was their father inviting them home with open arms.

Forgiveness. Who is waiting for yours?

Alan Cohen

Remember: 60 seconds of anger denies you 60 seconds of happiness. And it's your choice.

Ralph Waldo Emerson

Chapter 3 – Summary

Forgive, Forgive, Forgive

He that forgives and seeks reconcilement shall be recompensed by God. To endure with fortitude and to forgive is a duty incumbent on all.

Koran, Counsel 42:39,43

In the preceding pages, many visual definitions were given comparing anger to an acid, a poison, a hot coal that burns right through, devouring, distorting and destroying us. These visuals provide serious warnings as to anger's destructive power, a power that intensifies when we refuse to let go of it.

When we begin to understand that our anger toward others hurts *us* more than it hurts them, we can begin the process of refusing to allow it residence in our soul. Understanding anger's consequences also makes it easier, when we are tempted to become angry or to stay angry, to determine, "It's not worth it."

When we send out anger, more returns, multiplying unto itself until we become a vessel of resentment, bitterness and hate. However, no one has to live like this. No one. Each of us can, at any given moment, say, "Enough. No more."

If you are serious about addressing anger attitudes in your life, take a few minutes to do an anger assessment.

196

Honestly consider how often you "snap" at your spouse, your kids, your co-workers. Is it daily? Is it hourly? Does it take much to "set you off"? Remember as you reflect on these questions, that the attitudes we express on the outside are indicators as to what is going on in the inside. Many of us live our lives with a "fire down below," like volcanoes with the potential for eruption at any given moment, spewing out ashes.

Next, honestly consider how those who know you best would describe you. Would it be with words like "loving, gentle, understanding, kind"? Or would they have something else to say?

How about strangers? Do you readily curse at the fellow who cuts you off on the freeway? Can such an encounter ruin your whole morning? Or are you able to manage your reaction to the situation and manage your response?

How about telemarketers? Do you use these callers as verbal punching bags, slamming down the receiver on them? Or do you choose to end these calls promptly, yet with courtesy? Each reaction is an option available to us. One releases blessing, one withholds.

Managing our responses does not mean that we do not experience annoyance or frustration, but what it does mean is that these emotions are not handed a microphone and given center stage. We can choose to give voice to our every complaint, letting those in our path regularly have a piece of our mind, or we can choose, instead, attitudes that diminish and diffuse our anger. Forgiveness is one of these attitudes.

In the opening essay of this chapter, Saint Paul defined

love as meaning, among other things, not easily angered and keeping no record of wrongs. For those who desire to live a more loving life, these words are challenging, to say the least.

Paul urged his followers, as he does us, to be merciful and forgiving of others. But how do we do this? How does one begin the process of stepping away from our anger toward forgiveness? What is the key to making this possible?

It is my personal belief that Paul's readiness to forgive others was rooted in his understanding of human nature. He understood the necessity to forgive his fellow man by acknowledging his own shortcomings, and was more than aware of the ongoing spiritual battles we each face daily, battles sometimes won, and battles sometimes lost, battles waged moment by moment between the Light living within us and the Darkness living there as well, Good against Evil, our best selves against our worst.

It was this internal battle Paul spoke of in a letter he wrote to the church in Rome wherein he shared an agonizing explanation of the darkness that plagues us all. As you read the following, remember that these words belong to Saint Paul, anointed by God, a man responsible for writing the majority of the New Testament of the Christian Bible: "I do not understand what I do," wrote Paul. "For what I want to do I do not do, but what I hate I do. I know that nothing good lives in me, that is, in my sinful nature. For I have the desire to do what is good, but I cannot carry it out. For what I do is not the good I want to do; no, the evil I do not want to do – this I keep on doing. Now if I do what I do not want to do, it is no longer I who do it, but it is sin living in me that does it. So I find this law at work: When I want to do good, evil is right there with me. For in my inner being I delight in God's law; but I see another law at work in the members of my body, waging war against the law of my mind and making me a prisoner of the law of sin at work within my members. What a wretched man I am!" (Romans 7:14-15, 18-24)

Paul's words are filled with humility, and it is humility that paves the way for mercy. In understanding our own failings, we become more merciful toward the failings of others.

Know this: We are each Dr. Jekyll and we are each Mr. Hyde. We each have the power to enrich our life or the power to destroy it, each capable of the greatest evil or the greatest good – any one of us, at any time. We need to look no further than to the spiritual heroes of Scripture to know that this is true.

Consider Paul. He was capable of murder. So was Moses, who murdered as well. And then there is God's beloved King David who arranged for one of his trusted leaders to be killed because he had slept with this man's wife and now she was pregnant. Each of these men is remembered by history for the great good they did, but also for its opposite. The message of these examples, written down for eternity, instead of hidden away or denied, is this: Humans are a handful, and if we are of an opinion other than this, we have been living our lives with our eyes closed.

"Forgive," urged Paul again and again. "Forgive, forgive, forgive." His message never wavered and it never changed. Neither did his preaching for holiness, purity and righteousness. Despite Paul's failings, the intention of his heart was to try harder to be better, always striving for the higher ground of his soul.

We begin the process of forgiving others, first, by recognizing that the person we are holding animosity towards is loved by God and is an extension of the Divine, created in holiness, an image of the Almighty. Every single one of us owns holiness as our essence – even our enemies. It is easy to forget this when we are hurt. It is just as easy to forget that we, too, are Divine when we are making choices in our own lives that represent anything but. Let us remind ourselves always of who we are.

Second, we would do well to consider that the final word on David, Moses and Paul was not failure. Yes, each had failed, but, in the end, these men were not identified by those times when they were less than they could have been, or should have been.

Each of our lives is made up of strengths and weaknesses, spiritual victories and spiritual defeats, and if we wish for others to think of us in terms of what we have done well, instead of defining us by who we were in those times we fell short, then we must adopt this same attitude toward the errors and failings of our fellows.

"Blessed are the merciful," the Gospel of Matthew reminds us, "for they will be shown mercy." The circle is ever present, with mercy flowing from mercy, and grace giving birth to grace. Forgiveness then, as understood within the context of The Golden Formula, is more – much more – than a blessing we extend to another person, it is a blessing we extend unto ourselves.

We have a choice regarding forgiveness. Always, there comes a choice. We can choose to be forgiving of others, or we can choose not to be, and, as a result, live our lives with a heart turning to stone.

Life is fragile, our feelings so tender. To ask that we be forgiving of those who have caused us pain may seem an impossible task, as impossible as asking those whom we have pained for their forgiveness. No one denies this difficulty. Our legs may feel like granite as we take the first steps toward those persons who have hurt us, or toward those whom we have hurt. Our hand may shake as we extend it to another in peace or when we lift it to write the apology letter that is long overdue. Our voice may quiver when we speak the words "I am so very sorry" - or when we hear them spoken to us and respond, "You are forgiven." We may not even recognize it as our own.

Forgiveness. It is a required element of spiritual wellness. It encompasses both a willingness to be forgiving of those who admit they have hurt us, and a willingness to be forgiving of those who do not. Remember, the assassin who gunned down Gandhi was not standing over the great leader, as he lay there in the dust dying, saying, "I shouldn't have done that." Nor were the crowds beneath the cross telling Christ, "Sorry about those nails." No, there were no words of apology, only words of forgiveness. And those words were these: "Father, forgive them, for they know not what they do."

All the wishing in the world cannot take us back to yesterday to undo those things said, and those things done, that belong to another time. The wish cannot be granted.

But what can be granted is this: peace. Through forgiveness – the forgiving of others and the forgiving of ourselves – we can change, not what has gone before, but what is here, now, today, in this moment, and at this time.

And that is all that ever matters, because it is all that we ever have.

CHAPTER 4

Choosing an Attitude
Especially Gratitude

The Most Powerful Word in the World

Happiness doesn't depend upon who you are or what you have; it depends solely on what you think.

Dale Carnegie

Attitude. How important is it?

Charles Swindoll, writing in his compelling book, *Strengthening Your Grip*, gives this answer: "I believe the single most significant decision I can make on a day-to-day basis is my choice of attitude. It is more important than my past, my education, my bankroll, my successes or failures, fame or pain, what other people think of me or say about me, my circumstances, or my position. Attitude keeps me going or cripples my progress…It alone fuels my fire or assaults my hope. When my attitude is right, there's no barrier too high, no valley too deep, no dream too extreme, no challenge too great for me."

Is our attitude toward life really as significant as Swindoll would have us believe? Many among us would answer "yes" - like Emily. She's a vivacious high school senior who lives a couple hours drive from here. Not long ago, I interviewed her over breakfast for a local newspaper. The editors down at the paper thought her story would make for a great feature article. When I finished the interview, I couldn't agree more.

Here's what I learned about Miss Emily.

At first glance, you'd think this young lady has it all. She's bright, has a beautiful smile, and often laughs out loud. She was voted by her classmates as "Most Likely to Succeed" and was this Spring's prom queen. Really, you'd think she has it all.

Then you see the chair – the wheelchair, that is. For three years now, Emily has been confined to it. "Paralyzed from the waist down," were the words that changed her life.

Yet despite her challenges, she sat across from me smiling, ordered two eggs, and told me all about her life, her friends, and her dog named Pork Chop. I learned she likes to sing and she plans to go to college. Her favorite food is pizza, and her favorite color is yellow – "like sunshine and daffodils."

Where in the world does this girl's joy come from? I wondered.

If you ask her, she will tell you. She will tell you that it comes from her power to decide what thoughts will fill her mind. She will tell you that although the accident crippled her body, only she can cripple her mind – "and that would be the worst paralysis of all."

Attitude. It's powerful. It's also a choice. Day by day, we decide how we will greet each new morning and each new moment. Each decision is then subject to the same laws of multiplication that our actions are. By consistently sending out positive thoughts of gratitude, happiness and hopeful-ness, we connect with a positive energy that pulls like energy into our life. This is also true of the negative. Negative thinking multiplies upon itself and pulls more negative energy into our lives. For this reason alone, it is worth our time to evaluate what thoughts dominate our minds.

During the next week, try this. Pay close attention to your thoughts and, if time allows, write them down in a small notebook. Keep track of how often you find yourself thinking thoughts of gratitude and appreciation, and how often you find yourself in attitudes of criticism and complaining. Pay attention, as well, to the words you are speaking because they are an important indicator of the energy – positive or negative – that is presently the controlling force of your life.

If, at the end of the week, you find that you have been allowing negative thoughts to dominate your life and want to change this, start by replacing every negative thought with a positive one. Some days this will be easier than others, but through consistent efforts, this process will establish itself as a habit and positive responses will then become a more natural reaction.

In the daily grind of everyday life it is tempting to sit in the dark shadows of our thoughts and hit Life's rewind button, listening to yesterday's sad songs and singing, "Woe is me." There is no shortage of people who do this, and there is no shortage of those who would try to convince you that the sky is falling. We can find them at our jobs, in our neighborhoods, and sometimes they are even wearing our clothes and staring back at us when we look in the bathroom mirror in the morning.

If this is the case, let us consider accepting Life's invitation to step out of the shadows of our minds and come into the sunshine where we belong.

Positive thoughts are light. Negative thoughts are darkness. Nothing grows in the darkness. Not daffodils, and not us. Nature teaches us this in no uncertain terms. Light fosters warmth and growth, darkness fosters the exact opposite. When our thoughts are controlled by darkness and negativity, our hopes die, our dreams die, and our spirits die - contracting and closing in upon themselves. It takes just one second to change this. In the same single second it takes to walk into a dark room and throw the switch, flooding the room with light, we can summon a positive thought into our mind and dispel the darkness of negativity.

Emily agrees, and shares with me what she believes is the most powerful word in the world. The word is "next." It was this single word that helped her usher negative thoughts out of her mind after the accident, making room for something better.

She really is amazing and, at first glance, you would think she has it all. And do you know what? You'd be right. This young lady is living her life like she orders her eggs: "Sunny side up, please. Sunny side up."

A Lesson in Gratitude

The more you praise and celebrate in life, the more
there is in life to celebrate.

Oprah Winfrey

"Look for the good in life and you will find it." That may
seem like a Sunday school cliche' these days, but it is just as
true now as it ever was.

One man who believed it was Edward L. Kramer of St.
Louis, Missouri. Back in 1948 Kramer sought to teach this
principle to his three children.

He asked them to deliberately look each day for the
good in at least three people, people to whom they could be
thankful. "It can be in your playmates, your teachers - anyone with whom you come in contact with," he told them.

Each evening, after dinner, Kramer would sit down with
his children and ask them for an accounting of the good they
had found in people that day. Then postcards, expressing
their appreciation, were mailed to those individuals.

At first the children found the job difficult. But as they
began to train themselves to look for acts of kindness, trust,
and generosity, they found it easier and easier to do.

After a time, their thoughtfulness and their gratitude was
returned to them tenfold in the warmth and thankfulness of
the people who received the cards.

The family found themselves mailing so many thank

you notes that they decided to design their own card. It was patterned after the yellow telegram of Western Union. They called it a Thank-U-Gram.

Others heard of the family project and liked the idea so much that Kramer decided to offer a two week free supply to anyone who requested them.

During the next fifteen years or so, Kramer supplied people all over the country with millions of Thank-U-Grams. Such diverse people as President Eisenhower, Robert Frost, Leonard Bernstein, Bob Hope, Walt Disney, Henry Ford II, Jack Benny, and thousands upon thousands of others, both great and small, used Kramer's Thank-U-Grams - an idea that grew out of a father's desire to teach his children a moral principle about life.

The Best of Bits & Pieces

If we want a joyful life, we must think joyous thoughts. If we want a loving life, we must think loving thoughts. If we want a grateful life, we must think grateful thoughts. Whatever we send out mentally or verbally, will come back to us in like form.

Louise Hay

Thank You, God

Happiness is not a matter of good fortune or world-
ly possessions. It's a mental attitude. It comes from appreci-
ating what we have, instead of being miserable about what
we don't have. It's so simple – yet so hard for the human
mind to comprehend.

John Luther

I shall not mind the passage of the years so much for fear
of growing old if I have taken the time to cherish every
moment of my life. It won't matter to me if time moves on,
if, in its majestic passing, I've savored its most unremarked
upon gifts - if I've pondered a flowerbed of Forget-me-nots
blossoming so blue you'd think a piece of sky had fallen to
the earth.

If I have danced to the music of the night wind under a
starry sky and if I have seen the colors of the sunsets and
rainbows, if I have meditated long upon the thousand shades
of green that appear when Spring arrives in the valley and if
I've absorbed the hues of every flower I met along the dusty
roads, it will not matter quite so much should my eyes one
day grow dim.

If I've listened long to the subtle singing of bees among
the garden blooms and if I've laid awake at night when a
hush falls all around broken only by the whisper of the west
wind saying goodnight to the old cottonwood, if I've heard

211

a white-throated sparrow drop his song into the lap of a May morning and retain forever in my heart the memory of these melodies I have heard, then I won't mind so much when the long silence comes to stay and keeps me company teaching another way of listening. Live life in such a way and there will be no room for regrets.

How can one regret a single moment, or count life lost, if one has taken time to walk along a cliff's edge and watch a solitary gull soar into the arching sky that marks the pathways of infinity?

At dusk each evening, I pause in my day's tasks to see the Hand of God paint colors on the canvas of the sky. I look upward to behold and remember whatever masterpiece in this eternal present was prepared for my viewing, knowing that this sunset, this scene of chickadees in flight or cloud patterns evolving along the far horizon will never be quite the same as it is tonight. Tomorrow there will be different patterns, different shades and color tones, different vignettes to be savored, for within every sunrise and every sunset and every moment in between is a gift to be grateful for and a lesson to be learned. To be alive in the midst of so much that is wonderful is a blessing whose value is without measure.

And so, let us let thankfulness well up inside of our hearts and manifest its power in our everyday lives by making us more mindful and more humble; for it is gratitude that lifts our souls onto the summit of shining joy.

And because I want to look back and remember, I keep my own personal book of days in which for each day I have recorded at least one perfect moment of beauty I experienced in this small corner of the universe I call home. So, if someone were to ask me what I recall about any random date of the past year I can tell them on that day there was a sunset so splendid it turned all of creation to molten gold. Or on such a day I witnessed the unfolding of one perfect vermillion rose or saw yellow butterflies dancing in airy patterns to a music no human ear could detect. Or perhaps it was on such a day I heard a child laugh or saw a spider busy himself in the first gray light of dawn creating a perfect geometric design, lovely and flawless. In every moment of every day, beauty runs through life like a thread of silver song that links all of creation to the heart and mind of God.

The passage of days continues as it has always done, each bringing its blessing; each leaving its legacy to those who open their hearts to its bounty, pondering the magnitude of its miracles. Those who think themselves blessed indeed are the beneficiary of the benevolent companionship of the Infinite.

At twilight, I sing the song I've always sung. It never changes even though the years bring many changes. The song is still the same, "Deo Gracias." Thank you, God.

And today, I thank God for dew drops larger than diamonds clustered in the heart of a tulip blossom.

Margaret Jarek

The Power of Gratitude

I know it sounds terribly simplistic, but as I go about my day, I try to appreciate everything I see: a bird, a tree, a flower, something unusual happening. The more you notice the love, the miracles and the beauty around you, the more love comes into your life.

Betty Eadie

There is a wonderful Hasidic parable about the power of gratitude to change the course of our destiny in a heartbeat, the speed I imagine it takes for a "thank you" to reach heaven's ears.

Once, times were tough. Two men, both poor farmers, were walking down a country lane and met their Rabbi.

"How is it for you?" the Rabbi asked the first man.

"Lousy," he grumbled, bemoaning his lot and lack. "Terrible, hard, awful. Not worth getting out of bed for. Life is lousy."

Now God was eavesdropping on this conversation. "Lousy?" the Almighty thought. "You think your life is lousy *now*, you ungrateful lout. I'll show you what lousy is."

Then the Rabbi turned to the second man. "And you, my friend?"

"Ah, Rabbi, life is good. God is so gracious and so generous. Each morning when I awaken, I'm so grateful for the gift of another day for I know that, rain or shine, it will unfold in wonder and blessing too bountiful to count. Life is so good."

God smiled as the second man's thanksgiving soared upwards until it became one with the harmony of the heavenly host. Then the Almighty roared with a delighted laughter. "Good? You think your life is good *now*, I'll show you what good is!"

Gratitude is the most passionate, transformative force in the cosmos. When we offer thanks to God or to another human being, gratitude gifts us with renewal, reflection, reconnection.

Sarah Ban Breathnach

Be on the lookout for mercies. The more we look for them, the more of them we will see. Blessings brighten when we count them. Out of the determination of the heart, the eyes see. If you want to be gloomy, there's gloom enough to keep you glum. If you want to be happy, there's gleam enough to keep you glad. Better to lose count while naming your blessings than to lose your blessings by counting your troubles.

Maltbie D. Babcock

Learning Gratitude

Find the good. It's all around you. Find it, showcase it, and you'll start believing in it.

Jesse Owens

We can be governed by our admirations rather than our dislikes. We can concentrate so much on things for which we are grateful that there's no time to focus on gloom.

When I was a boy, we sang an old hymn with the refrain "Count your many blessings, name them one by one." It is one of the best ways to divest yourself of the negative: to consciously enumerate things for which you are grateful.

When you are feeling sorry for yourself, Dale Carnegie recommends that you take out pencil and paper and make a list of all the good things you have, despite your problems.

Good advice!

Alan Loy McGinnis

Four Magic Words

When it comes to life the critical thing is whether you take things for granted or take them with gratitude.

G. K. Chesterton

A legend tells about a servant whose master died - leaving the servant a bag of blessings - full to its brim. "The bag will always be full," said the master, "so long as you remember the four magic words."

As the servant started off on his merry way, he partook of the blessings in the bag until finally the bag was almost empty. He then sought desperately to remember the words. Asking a man nearby what the four words might be, he was told, "Perhaps the words are 'I wish I had.'"

So, with his nearly empty bag, he ran down the road shouting: "I wish I had! I wish I had as much as all my neighbors have of health and wealth and such!"

But still the bag held no more. Some distance farther along the way, he asked another person, "Can you please tell me what the magic words are that will restore blessings to the bag?"

This person said, "Perhaps the four words are 'Give me some more.'"

So once again he started on his way, shouting to the skies: "Give me some more! Give me some more! Oh, fill my bag of blessings up as full as it was before!"

Still the bag remained empty. Lonely and dejected, he sat down along a roadway to take the last piece of bread from his bag. As he started to eat it, a small child came up to him and - out of hunger - asked the man for a piece of bread. It was the last piece he had, but he gave it to the child, forgetting his own hunger. The little one placed the bread down before eating it, folded his hands, and said, "I thank Thee, Lord."

The servant jumped up with excitement to say, "Those are the words! Those are the words!" He took his empty bag and literally ran down the road shouting: "I thank Thee, Lord! I thank Thee, Lord! I thank Thee, Lord, once more for all the blessings in my bag. O Lord, how great a store!"

And the bag of blessings was full once more.

Glenn Van Ekeren

The Richness of Life's Simple Pleasures

There are things in life that won't cost you a penny,
but the rewards they reap are worth their weight in gold.
They won't cost you a dime, but I guarantee you'll feel like
a million for the time well spent.

Kathy Whirity

Laura Ingalls Wilder wrote, *"I am beginning to learn that it is the sweet simple things of life which are the real ones after all."* I couldn't agree more. Here are a few of mine:

Bouncing a baby on my knee, driving up the coast, ordering the "catch of the day" in a harbor town cafe, seeing white picket fences, wearing bib overalls and flannel shirts in fall, skinny dipping in the moonlight, sliding down banisters, reading a long novel on a short weekend, believing in miracles, dining by candlelight - even if it's only over a grilled cheese sandwich and bowl of tomato soup, spotting the first robin in Spring, hearing my children call "nitey nite" from their bedrooms down the hall, sitting in the old wicker rocker on my front porch, keeping a teddy bear handy, smelling my mother's pies, eating them, too, singing Ald Lange Syne on New Year's Eve, attending ice cream socials and poetry readings, walking down cobblestone pathways, being asked to dance, feeling the rush of blood to my cheeks when I say, "Yes," doodling, reading old love letters, hearing the conversations of frogs from across the marsh at dusk, counting the spots on the back of a lady bug, cross country skiing, playing frisbee with my dog, finding a nickel in my pocket when passing a bubble gum machine, pondering God, hearing a barbershop quartet, experiencing a night of peaceful slumber, finding a blue M&M, riding ferris wheels, hanging a "Do Not Disturb" sign on my hotel room door (ahhhhhhhhhhh vacation), giving a toddler a horsie ride, feeling my heart fill with the helium of hope when I look to the future, spending the middle of a summer afternoon in the middle of an inner tube in the middle of a pond, setting a bouquet of lilac blossoms on my bedside bureau in the Springtime, visiting an apple orchard in September, hearing someone whistle, listening to an oldies station on the radio, ice skating a figure 8, wondering what those jello wrestling tournaments are all about, painting my toe nails geranium red, seeing smoke rise from a neighbor's chimney on a cool autumn day, tasting the firsts of the season (all of them: the first strawberry, the first watermelon, the first peach, the first ear of corn), hearing a banjo played live, and sitting on the end of a pier watching fish jump.

Total cost: almost nothing. Total value: priceless.

Just think how happy you would be if you lost everything and everyone you have right now, and then, somehow got everything back again.

Kobi Yamada

The Driving Force of My Survival

Hold on to the good.
I Thessalonians 5:21

Gerta Weissman was among the prisoners in a Nazi death camp. She recalled an episode when she and her fellow inmates stood at roll call for hours on end, nearly collapsing with hunger and fatigue. But they noticed in the corner of that bleak, horrid, gray place that the concrete had broken and a flower had poked its head through. The thousands of woman there took great pains to avoid stepping on it. It was the only spot of beauty in their ugly and heinous world, and they were thankful for it.

Later in a radio interview, she added: "When people ask me, 'Why did you go on?' there is only one picture that comes to mind. The moment was when I stood at the window of the first camp I was in and asked myself, if by some miraculous power one wish could be granted me, what would it be? And then, with almost crystal clarity, the picture that came to my mind was a picture of my home - my father smoking his pipe, my mother working at her needlepoint, my brother and I doing our homework. And I remember thinking, my goodness, it was just a regular evening at home. I had known countless evenings like that. And I knew at that moment that this picture would be for me the driving force of my survival."

Robert J. Morgan

Surrender to Negative or Strive for Positive

The greatest discovery of our generation is that human beings can alter their lives by altering the attitudes of their mind.

William James

In this life, attitude is everything.

Not only is it the single element in our lives over which we are at liberty to exercise complete control, but it will be the sole determinant of the quality of our lives.

Now there are a few among us who seem to be born with a good attitude, but for most of us, developing and maintaining an ability to believe firmly in the power of good is a work in process.

I suppose one might say I experienced a kind of an epiphany when I was in sixth grade. We had the word "pessimist" added to our weekly vocabulary. One of my schoolmates, who rather took delight in her feelings of superiority over the rest of us, turned to me and announced in a voice heard throughout the classroom, "That's what you are Margaret, a pessimist."

I was taken aback. No ready retort came to mind. I was too busy searching through the files of my mind trying to determine the truth or fallacy of that statement. I am still working on it.

The moment stood out in my mind over the years

because it was instrumental in propelling me toward an understanding that I, not the circumstances of my life, was going to determine what kind of life I would live.

A bright and positive outlook has not been something I attained instantaneously. By no means was I born an optimist, nor did I come endowed with a naturally upbeat personality. So to remain positive and optimistic is a full-time-operation. Moment by moment, I must make a choice whether I will surrender to the negative or strive for the positive.

Some days I need to be my own sunshine when the clouds thicken. Some days I need to be my own springtime when life's wintry moments come along. But in the end, the light must overcome the darkness and my world as I perceive it must begin within my own thoughts. Never easy, always a challenge, the role of being an optimist is a role one must exert a constant series of choices. It's those choices, made one-by-one, that ultimately heal our lives, our wounds, and the wounds of the world.

Negativity is by far the easiest attitude in the world to possess. It takes no more effort to slide into negativity than it takes to fall off a log. It's about as easy as standing in quicksand and simply allowing it to have its way. But each of us must continually, consciously, and determinedly choose to transcend such attitudes. This is the greatest challenge any of us will ever encounter. Taking command over one's natural reactions and thought tendencies takes constant vigilance and a surprising amount of self-discipline. Events around us, difficult as they may be, act as catalysts, forcing us to make the choice between the positive and the negative every moment of every day.

From a spiritual perspective, life is an adventure in which every moment holds a thousand choices, and we ourselves become the troubadours who recite the story of our own life's journey upward toward the light.

So fill your mind with lovely thoughts to keep the deep shadows at bay. The more you allow yourself to believe in loveliness, the more loveliness will appear. Hallow out a place in your heart to which you can retreat and be at peace even if the outer world is not.

Margaret Jarek

How We Look at Things

The greater part of our happiness or misery depends on our disposition and not on our circumstances.

Martha Washington

There is a story of identical twins. One was a hope-filled optimist. "Everything is coming up roses!" he would say. The other was a sad and hopeless pessimist.

The worried parents of the boys brought them to the local psychologist. He suggested to the parents a plan to balance the twins' personalities. "On their next birthday," he told them, "Put them in separate rooms to open their gifts. Give the pessimist the best toys you can afford, and give the optimist a box of manure."

The parents followed these instructions and carefully observed the results.

When they peeked in on the pessimist, they heard him audibly complaining, "I don't like the color of this computer...I'll bet this calculator will break...I don't like this game...I know someone who's got a bigger toy car than this one..."

Tiptoeing across the corridor, the parents peeked in and saw their little optimist gleefully throwing the manure up in the air. He was giggling. "You can't fool me! Where there's this much manure, there's gotta be a pony!"

As cited in *The Sower's Seeds*
by Brian Cavanaugh

227

A Philosophy for Life

Keep your thoughts POSITIVE
because your thoughts become your words.

Keep your words POSITIVE
because your words become your actions.

Keep your actions POSITIVE
because your actions become your habits.

Keep your habits POSITIVE
because your habits become your values.

Keep your values POSITIVE
because your values become your destiny.
Mahatma Gandhi

There is little difference in people, but that little difference makes a big difference. The little difference is attitude. The big difference is whether it is positive or negative.

Clement Stone

As You Think

There exists the Law of the Fallow Field. Simply stated, this Law holds that if nothing positive is planted in the garden, it will always revert to weeds. So, we have to continually plant each growing season exactly what it is we expect to grow. If nothing of value is planted, nothing of value will be harvested.

Brian Cavanaugh

Your mind may be likened to a garden that may be intelligently cultivated or allowed to run wild - but whether cultivated or neglected, it must, and will, bring forth. If no useful seeds are put into it, then an abundance of useless weed seeds will fall therein, and will continue to produce their kind.

Just as gardeners cultivate their plots, keeping them free from weeds, and growing the flowers and fruits they desire, so may you tend the garden of your mind, weeding out all the wrong, useless, and impure thoughts, and cultivating toward perfection the flowers and fruits of right, useful, and pure thoughts. By pursuing this process, you will sooner or later discover that you are the master gardener of your soul, the director of your life. You also reveal, within yourself, the laws of thought, and understand, with ever-increasing accuracy, how the forces of thought and elements of the mind operate in the shaping of your character, circumstances, and destiny.

You are where you are by the law of your being; the thoughts that you have built into your character have brought you there, and in the arrangement of your life there is no element of chance, but all is the result of a law that cannot err.

And so we are held prisoners only by ourselves: Our own thoughts and actions are the jailers of our fate - they imprison, if they are base; they are also the angels of freedom - they liberate, if they are noble.

Most of us are anxious to improve our circumstances, but are unwilling to improve ourselves - and we therefore remain bound. If we do not shrink from honest self-examination we can never fail to accomplish the object our hearts are set upon.

Good thoughts and actions can never produce bad results; bad thoughts and actions can never produce good results. We understand this law in the natural world, and work with it; but few understand it in the mental and moral world - although its operation there is just as simple and undeviating.

To live continually in thoughts of ill will, cynicism, suspicion, and envy, is to be confined in a self-made prison cell. But to think well of all, to be cheerful with all, to patiently learn to find the good in all - such unselfish thoughts are the very portals of heaven. To dwell day by day in thoughts of peace toward every creature will bring abounding peace to their possessor.

James Allen

Choosing Your Mindset

Attitude: It is our best friend or our worst enemy.
John C. Maxwell

A young midwestern lawyer had a dark side to his nature in his early years. On one occasion his friends thought it wise to keep knives and razors out of his reach and to have someone stay with him through the night. During this period, the tormented man wrote, "I am now the most miserable man living. If what I feel were equally distributed to the whole human family, there would not be one cheerful face on earth. Whether I shall ever be better I cannot tell; I awfully forebode I shall not. To remain as I am is impossible; I must die or be better, it appears to me."

Those words were written in 1841 by Abraham Lincoln. His law partner, William Hearndon, said that "melancholy dripped from him as he walked" during that period.

But note how different he sounds in 1863: "The year that is drawing toward the close," President Lincoln wrote, "has been filled with the blessings of fruitful fields and healthful skies. These bounties are so constantly enjoyed that we are prone to forget the source from which they come." He was painfully aware that thousands of America's young men were dying in the Civil War and that the country could be on the brink of collapse, but he was still able to see the goodness around him.

Sometime between 1841 and 1863, Lincoln had evidently learned certain habits of mind that enabled him to put much of his despairing tendencies behind him. Not that he became carefree and blithely happy in those years when the Republic shuddered; he would have been less a man had he suffered less. But he acquired an ability to live in the midst of tragedy and still cultivate qualities like gratitude and joy. A clue to Lincoln's character may lie in a remark he once made to someone on the subject. "I've noticed," said Lincoln, "that most people are about as happy as they make up their minds to be."

Alan Loy McGinnis

Granny's Glasses

Make the most of the best and the least of the worst.
Robert Louis Stevenson

A little boy said to his playmate, "When I get older, I want to wear glasses just like Granny's because she can see so much more than most people. She can see the good in a person when everyone else sees a bad side. She can see what a person meant to do even if he or she didn't do it. I asked her one day how she could see the good, and she said it was the way she learned to look at things as she got older. And when I get older, I want a pair of glasses just like Granny's so I can see the good, too."

How different our world would be if we all wore a pair of Granny's glasses! If I would look for the good in you, and you would look for the good in me, our lives would be so much more pleasant.

At times, we are like the buzzard that seeks out what is rotten and ugly, when we should be like the hummingbird that looks for what is sweet and beautiful.
Walter Buchanan

How delightful is the company of joyful people, who overlook trifles and keep their minds instinctively fixed on whatever is good and positive in the world about them. They feed on the true and beautiful wherever they find it. And what is more, they find it everywhere.

Van Wyck Brooks

What Do You See?

What you see reflects your thinking, and your think-ing but reflects your choice of what you want to see.

A Course in Miracles

The story has been retold countless times in countless ways over the last many centuries. It happened like this: A traveler approached a great, walled city. Before entering its gates, he stopped to talk with an old man seated beneath a tree.

"What are the people like in this city?" asked the traveler.

"How were the people from where you came?" wondered the old man.

"A terrible lot," grumbled the traveler. "Mean, miserable, and detestable in all respects."

"You will find them here the same," responded the old man.

A second traveler soon happened by. He, too, was on his way to the great city and stopped to ask the old man about the people he would soon meet there.

The old man repeated the question he had asked the first traveler: "How were the people from where you came?"

To this the second traveler answered, "They were fine people. Generous, kind, compassionate."

"You will find them here the same," observed the old man.

Be Happy Where You Are

We see things not as they are, but as we are.
Anais Nin

On an airplane recently I made the mistake of admitting to the woman next to me that I'm in the psychology business. "Oh," she said. "You're just the one I want to talk to. My husband is completely dissociated from reality."

For the next hour she told me how much she hated Los Angeles and how she was trying to get her husband to make the break and move with her to Ketchum, Idaho. She hated LA's smog, and she hated its culture. The crime was disgraceful, the traffic was awful, nobody was friendly, everyone was out to cheat you, and the people moving into her neighborhood were riffraff.

She was a nice enough lady, and I hope she'll be happy in Ketchum, but I've noticed that those who are miserable in LA are usually miserable in Ketchum as well.

On the other hand, those who believe that love is the greatest power we possess find things to enjoy in the people around them regardless of the locale.

Alan Loy McGinnis

All These Things

*There is the positive side and the negative side and
at every moment I decide.*

William James

In *A Turtle on a Fencepost,* Allan Emery tells of accompanying businessman Ken Hansen to visit a hospitalized employee. The patient lay very still, his eyes conveying anguish. His operation had taken eight hours, and recovery was long and uncertain.

"Alex," said Ken quietly, "you know I have had a number of serious operations. I know the pain of trying to talk. I think I know what questions you're asking. There are two verses I want to give you—Genesis 42:36 and Romans 8:28. We have the option of these two attitudes. We need the perspective of the latter."

Hansen turned to the passages, read them, then prayed and left. The young man, Alex Balc, took the message to heart. He later enjoyed a full recovery.

Every day we choose one of these attitudes amid life's difficulties—to be beat-up, or to be up-beat. To say with Jacob in Genesis 42:36: All these things are against me. Or to say with Paul in Romans 8:28: All these things are working together for good to those who love the Lord.

Robert J. Morgan

The Wooden Sword

What the mind dwells on, expands.
Norman Vincent Peale

Once there was a king whose worrisome thoughts swirled around his head like a storm. He feared that his armies would lose battles, fretted that his treasury would one day be empty, and suspected that his ministers were disloyal. He had no peace.

One day as the king stood at his window, gazing at the crowds in the marketplace beyond the palace walls, he wondered, "How do common people find happiness? Do they worry as much as I do?" He sighed and said to himself, "I wish I were a bird who could fly off and listen to their daily conversations."

Suddenly, the king's eyes brightened with an idea. He called his servants to bring him the crudest cloth they could find. He ordered royal seamstresses to assemble a suit of rags and a hooded cloak. When servants delivered these clothes to the royal chamber, the king sent everyone away and eyed the rough attire. Standing before his mirror, he carefully removed his crown, smudged his face with ashes, and dressed himself in the ragged clothes. He appeared every bit a beggar. Pleased with this disguise, he crept from the palace. Even the guards did not recognize him.

The disguised king walked freely through the crowds in

239

the bazaar all day, observing the ways of common people. It was nightfall when he passed a rundown cottage at the edge of the city. Peeking through the window, the king saw a man sitting at a crude wooden table, eating a loaf of bread. The man's smile lit up the dingy room. The king eyed the meal and the humble surroundings. He wondered, "Why is this poor man so happy?" Unable to quell his curiosity, the king knocked on the door.

"I am a poor beggar," the king said in his humblest voice. "Can you spare some food?"

"Certainly!" said the poor man. "A guest is always a welcome blessing in this house. I do not have much, but what I have is yours."

The poor man's generosity dumbfounded the king. After the two seated themselves, the poor man blessed and cut the bread. The king accepted a share of the loaf and watched the man gaily chew the bread as if it were the finest meal.

"Why are you so happy?" the king asked.

The poor man replied, "It was a good day! I am a cobbler who repairs old shoes. Today I fixed enough shoes to earn a loaf of bread."

"But what if tomorrow you do not earn your bread?" the king inquired.

The poor man looked deep into the king's eyes. He saw how the strain of worry had furrowed his brow. The poor man smiled and simply replied, "Day by day, I have faith. All will be well."

The king mused over these words and thought to himself, "This man's faith brings him happiness. He is naive. I wonder how happy he would remain in times of difficulty." The king left the cottage planning to test the man's faith.

The next morning when the man went out to ply his trade as a cobbler, he discovered that the king had issued a new law. A sign in the marketplace read, "It is henceforth illegal for anyone to repair shoes. When shoes wear out, people must buy new ones."

The poor man sighed and assured himself, "All will be well." He glanced about the market and noticed an old woman struggling with a bucket of water at the well. He rushed to assist her, and for his trouble, she handed him a coin. As the poor man fingered the coin in his hand, his faith in the future shone brightly. He carried water for people all day and by sunset had enough money to buy himself dinner.

Curious to see if his new friend could be happy without a meal, the king - again disguised as a beggar - returned to the poor man's house. To his surprise, through the window he saw the man eating bread and drinking a glass of wine.

He knocked on the door, and the poor man brought him immediately to the table. The king asked, "How is it that tonight you drink wine and eat bread? I have seen the new law posted in the market, so surely you did not fix shoes today!"

"No, indeed, I did not," explained the poor man. "Today I earned more than before by carrying water for people. The loss of my first profession has made room for my new one!"

"What if no one wants you to carry water tomorrow?" asked the king.

The poor man looked into the king's eyes and simply

replied, "Day by day, I have faith. All will be well."

The king left the cottage, bewildered by the poor man's faith. "He has not tasted hard times," thought the king.

The next day when the poor man went to the well, he saw that the king had made yet another new law. The king's messengers posted a sign on the well: "It is now illegal for anyone to carry water for others."

The poor man considered this predicament for a moment and looked about the marketplace. He noticed men carrying wood from the forest on their backs. He approached a woodcutter and asked if he needed an assistant.

"Certainly!" was the reply, and the poor man spent the day cutting and carrying wood to market. By nightfall, he had earned enough to buy bread, wine, and cheese for his dinner.

When the king, again dressed as a beggar, arrived at the cottage, the poor man invited him to come inside. To the king's surprise, the poor man shared an even finer meal.

"How did you earn your keep today?" inquired the king.

"I am a woodcutter now," said the poor man, smiling broadly. "As I told you, I have faith. As you can see, things are getting better all the time!"

The king grumbled as he left the cottage. "I must be far more clever in testing this man. Surely when he cannot buy food for his belly, his faith will waver."

The next day when the poor man went to join the other woodcutters, he found them surrounded by palace soldiers. The captain loudly announced, "The king has commanded that all woodcutters must report to the palace gate to become guards."

The captain shuffled the poor man off with the rest. The poor man, now dressed stiffly in a colorful uniform with a sharp sword in a sheath at his side, stood guard all day at the palace gate. As the sun set, he went to the captain of the soldiers to request some pay so that he could buy his evening meal.

"Palace guards are paid once a month," the captain curtly replied.

With a sigh, the poor man set out for home. As he passed the pawnshop, an idea came to him. He sold the metal blade of the sword for enough money to buy food for a month. "With what I earn by the end of the month as a guard," he thought, "I can easily buy back the sword and return it to its rightful place."

The poor man rushed home and set the table with a fine meal. Before he ate, however, he busied himself carving a wooden blade to fill the now empty sheath he would wear at his side the next day.

The king, once again disguised in rags, returned to the cottage and saw the food on the table. "How did you buy this food?" he asked in amazement, knowing that the man could not possibly have earned any money that day. The poor man explained, "I sold the metal blade of the sword for enough money to buy food for a month."

Never suspecting that the ragged beggar who stood before him was in fact the king, the poor man showed the wooden blade he was carving. "This will replace the blade I sold until I earn enough money to buy it back again."

"That is not so clever of you," said the king. "What if you must draw your sword tomorrow?"

Once again the poor man just replied, "Day by day, I have faith. All will be well."

"I have him now!" the king chuckled under his breath as he left the cottage. "His faith will not be so strong in the dungeon!"

The next day the poor man stood in uniform once again, guarding the palace gate. The captain of the king's soldiers, followed by a noisy crowd, dragged a man accused of being a thief. The captain led the thief up to the poor man at the palace gate and gruffly said, "This thief has stolen a melon. The king has ordered that you cut off his head."

The thief begged for mercy. He fell to his knees weeping. "Please do not kill me! I had no food and my children were hungry."

The poor man, guarding the gate, stood tall in his uniform and calmly considered the awkward situation. He thought, "If I pull out my sword to kill this man, I, too, will be beheaded. Everyone will see that the royal blade is missing!" He pondered a bit more and then solemnly reminded himself, "All will be well."

As the large crowd watched, he lifted his arms to the heavens and cried out, "Blessed be the Most High! If this man is truly guilty, give me the strength to serve the king's command. But if this man is not," he said, gripping the handle of the sword at his side, "let the blade of my sword be turned to wood!" Dramatically, he drew his wooden sword and thrust it high above his head. A gasp went through the crowd. "It's a miracle!" the people exclaimed.

Immediately, the man accused of theft was set free.

At that moment, out of the crowd stepped the king. He approached the poor man in the guard uniform and said, "Do you recognize me?"

The man replied, "You are the king."

"No," replied the king, "I am the beggar whom you fed each night."

The poor man's face spread with a smile, for he recognized the king's furrowed brow.

The king smiled in return and said, "Tonight and every night, my friend, you will dine with me! Your light of faith can help me chase away my dark fears of the future."

And so it came to pass that the man, who owned little but was rich in faith, became the wise and trusted adviser to the king.

Heather Forest

Offer Kind Words

Happiness is contagious. Be a carrier.
Robert Orben

Have you ever noticed what happens when you say something nice to someone - "That's a beautiful shirt." "You did a great job." "Thank you for coming into my life!" - it's like pouring water on a wilted plant! No matter what is going on, immediately the recipient perks up. Her face glows, a smile appears, and she looks like the weight of the world is off her shoulders, if only for a moment.

The other day I was walking back to work from lunch with my head down, brooding over my own misery, and I ran smack into a tiny old man coming out of a store and knocked him down. I was so embarrassed I could hardly speak. He picked himself up, smiled at me, and said, "Thank you, young lady, that's more excitement than I've had in months." It was so unexpected, I burst out laughing, and he smiled again. As he was walking away, he turned back to me and said, "You have a very beautiful laugh, use it often."

The Practice of Kindness

...whatever is true, whatever is noble, whatever is right, whatever is pure, whatever is lovely, whatever is admirable – if anything is excellent or praiseworthy – think about such things... and the God of peace will be with you.

Philippians 4:8-9

Chapter 4 – Summary

Unleashing Gratitude's Power

Let a man purify his thoughts, for what a man thinks, that he is; this is the eternal mystery. Man becomes that of which he thinks.

Upanishads

There is a Biblical story that sums up the ideas discussed in this chapter. Particularly, it is a story that provides a powerful example of the importance of choosing an attitude of gratitude. It reads:

Jesus called his disciples to him and said, "I have compassion for these people; they have already been with me three days and have nothing to eat. I do not want to send them away hungry or they may collapse on the way."

His disciples answered, "Where could we get enough bread in this remote place to feed such a crowd?"

"How many loaves do you have?" Jesus asked.

"Seven," they replied, "and a few small fish."

He told the crowd to sit down on the ground. Then he took the seven loaves and the fish and when he had given thanks, he broke them and gave them to the disciples, and they in turn to the people. They all ate and were satisfied. Afterward the disciples picked up seven basketfuls of broken pieces that were left over. The number of those who ate was

248

four thousand, besides women and children. (Matthew 15:32-38)

There are two opposing attitudes present in the story above: the attitude of gratitude displayed by Christ and the hopeless attitude of the disciples asking, "Where could we get enough bread in this remote place to feed such a crowd?"

The attitude of the disciples was a repeat of the attitude they had shown earlier in Jesus' ministry when he fed another large crowd totaling 5,000. When the disciples were asked at that time how much food was available, they preceded the total accounting of food with the words, "We have here only."

"Only" is a word of defeat, a word of lack – not a word of power. That's why Christ didn't use it. Instead, he chose language of thankfulness and focused on what he did have, not on what he didn't. Taking the loaves and fish into his hands, he paused and gave thanks. Then, behold, a miracle.

We, too, can begin the process of thankfulness as discussed in this chapter and release gratitude's miraculous power into our own lives. For what we have at this moment, let us say, "Thank you."

As we make it a habit to regularly participate in attitudes of gratitude, we discover that gratefulness begins multiplying itself into our heart like the miraculous loaves and fishes of long ago, showering spiritual abundance - contentment, awe and joy – into our life like a rainstorm into the desert. Our own choices turn the faucets of heaven on or our own choices shut them off.

Does heaven really seek our thankfulness? Does gratefulness really matter?

I believe the answer to these questions is found in another short Biblical teaching that accounts the healing of ten lepers.

After being miraculously cleansed of their diseases, one of these men returned to Christ to express his gratitude. Just one. Christ's response to the man who returned was this: "Were not all ten cleansed? Where are the other nine?"

It was a pointed question and it evidenced dismay. "Where are the other nine?" Jesus wondered, and then he followed up that question with this one: "Was no one found to return and give praise to God except this foreigner?"

Christ's words clearly show a God who desires our thankfulness.

Take a moment to personally reflect on where you see yourself in these teachings. Is gratitude a regular part of your life? Are you ready to respond to Life with a "thank you" or are you more like the missing nine?

Consider the disciples on the hillside as well. Does your thinking mirror theirs? Are you typically a person who is prone to see the negative side of life or are you a person who is on the lookout for miracles in everyday moments?

If your life is presently prone to the negative, you can change it. In the same way you can make the decision to train your body into fitness when you are out-of-shape, you can make the decision to train your mind into healthy thinking. The law of cause and effect works the same in the unseen spiritual world of thinking as it does in the physical world, and that law states this: effort yields results.

Common sense tells us that if we continually eat junk, we will experience a result from these choices and become sick. The same principle works for our minds. If we continually choose "junk" thoughts, we experience a result from these choices and become "sick" in the realm of our thinking. And ultimately, this can be manifested from our minds into our flesh through the unity of our being as one body, mind and spirit.

Would you eat meat that has been lying on the kitchen cupboard for a week and has turned rancid? Of course not! Would you drink from a bottle marked "poison"? Of course not! Common sense tells us not to eat or drink anything impure because it will result in sickness to our flesh. We understand this concept very well in the physical world, but the same truth holds for our minds. We must refuse impure thoughts access into our beings in the same way we would refuse poison. Each of us chooses what we will eat and drink – healthy or unhealthy – and each of us chooses what we will think – healthy or unhealthy. Negative thoughts of hate, bitterness, anger, prejudice, self-pity, lust, criticism, gossip and the like, contaminate our thinking. Then, they contaminate our lives.

The closing quotation in this chapter is delivered as a command: "Whatever is true, whatever is noble, whatever is right, whatever is pure, whatever is lovely, whatever is admirable – if anything is excellent or praiseworthy – think about such things."

These words are to be the measuring rod of our thoughts, and they have a payoff: it is peace. Let us make every effort to fill our minds with that which is true and noble, pure and lovely, admirable and excellent, and all things praiseworthy. In doing so, we shall bring on the rains of blessing.

You can get started on your journey toward blessing by making the commitment to seek beauty in the world around you and to seek beauty in its people.

Focus your thoughts and attitudes on the positive aspects of life as often as possible. Train yourself to think regularly about the positive points of your job, your family, and your life. As you make it a habit to replace negatives with positives, you will begin to see the good in life, not the bad. You will begin to see the strengths within others, not the weaknesses. This does not mean that the weaknesses will not exist, or that the world is void of its darkness which includes the darkness within each of us, but rather, what it does mean is that even though we understand that darkness exists always, we also understand that light does too - and we can choose to see it always.

Consider getting a role model. Choose a person who you believe displays an upbeat, cheerful attitude. Look for someone who possesses personality qualities you would like to develop in your own life. Then, start paying attention to their words. Give careful thought to the subjects they choose to talk about.

Next, start paying close attention to your own words as you work to rid yourself of the negative – or at least reduce its presence in your life. Consider the subjects you spend the majority of your time thinking about and talking about. Are you regularly conversing about everything that is wrong with the world and its people or do you choose to speak of the true and beautiful?

At work, are you one of the chronic complainers who is always ready to find fault with their job, their supervisor and their company? If so, remember this: no one is blessed by those persons who carry these attitudes. Specifically, the person who carries these attitudes is not blessed.

This does not mean we cannot discuss the challenges that face us and address legitimate concerns in a respectable manner. There is no harm in addressing problems when we are focusing on the positive choices that can be made that will lead us toward a solution. However, there is great harm to be realized by repeatedly talking about our problems if it is not in terms of how we intend to fix them. We will only increase our problems and root them into our lives deeper by continuing to do nothing more than focus on the negative.

Lastly, practice gratitude. Spend some time daily reflecting on how you would answer this question: What am I grateful for?

You can do this while driving to work, while taking your morning walk or by journaling your gratitude before bedtime. Whether this time of reflection comes in the morning, at noon, or at night is not important. What matters most is that you do not let the day close without having an answer to that question.

Be ever in search of thankfulness.

CHAPTER 5

I Believe!

Aspire Higher

The starting point of achievement is desire. Keep this constantly in mind. Weak desires bring weak results, just as a small amount of fire makes a small amount of heat.

Napoleon Hill

We know the story, the childhood favorite about a little railroad steam engine that encountered a great mountain along its way and was unable to go on. The steam engine wouldn't go on because it believed it couldn't go on. It thought the mountain was too high, and it thought itself too little. And as long as the steam engine believed this, it was true.

So there the engine stayed, on the tracks below the mountain, staring up to the peak from down below, afraid, until it got to thinking that the summit could be reached if only he tried. Four words later, the wheels below him started turning. Those words were, "I think I can." It was this belief that moved the little locomotive upward, and this same belief that set his engine to roaring, propelling him over the mountain and into the world beyond. The little steam engine thought he could, and so he did. He believed, and so he achieved.

We, too, can reach for the summits of our life and fulfill our dreams by using the same circle principle that promises us more love, more joy and more peace in our lives. All of life hinges to The Formula. Just as love brings love and joy brings joy, positive belief in our ability to fulfill our dreams triggers positive results. Before we can achieve, we must first believe.

Never doubt for a single second that your dreams are reachable. You can reach them because they lie within your own heart.

Here, within our hearts, we also encounter our mountains – mountains of fear and doubt that would convince us otherwise. Just as positive thinking is a power, so is fear. And the time comes when each of us must decide what it is we will be made of. We hold the power to choose to believe in the mountains that stand in our way or in the miracle that is waiting to be our life. Which will it be?

There is a world that awaits us on the other side of self-doubt, a world that only we can take ourselves to. When we come against our fears with the power of positive faith and positive hope, these mountains cease to be victorious over us and we discover that they're not so big after all.

What is it you hope for? What is it you dream? Today, spend a few moments thinking about your answers to these questions. Then carefully examine your thoughts regarding your dreams. Do you find yourself more often believing "I can't do it" or believing the opposite perspective of "Yes, I can!"? Pay close attention to your thoughts. It is worth your while to do so because your perspective directly and pro-foundly influences the realization of everything you hope for. The world you determine to build around you is first built within. We live our lives from the inside out - every single one of us. We may have different dreams from one another, different destinations to arrive at, but we travel the same path on our way to them, the pathway through our heart. And along this path we come to realize that the only obstacle that can ever stand in our way is ourselves.

Know this: There isn't a place in the whole wide world that someone else can go to that you cannot. There isn't a dream your heart is hoping for that someone else can achieve and you will be denied. Do you believe this? It matters if you do. It matters very much.

A great promise was delivered to mankind two thousand years ago by One sent from God, a great promise that lies in a single sentence. What sentence? This one: "All things are possible to him who believes." The message was not "some" things, and it was not "many" things. The message was "all." *All* things are possible. Possible for who? Possible for the one who believes. Is this you?

When your answer becomes "yes," you will know it – and others will, too. They will hear in your voice and see in your eyes that the engine of hope has started to roar in your soul.

Then, there will be but one thing left for you to do: fasten your seatbelt because you're about to head straight up the side of a mountain.

When your heart is in your dream, no request is too extreme.

Jiminy Cricket

Surmounting Life's Peaks

Don't be afraid. Just believe.
Mark 5:36

The next time you're faced with a seemingly insurmountable task, consider the hurdles Erik Weihermayer has overcome.

Erik has worked as a middle-school teacher, run marathons, and performed acrobatic skydiving stunts. He's also a scuba diver, downhill skier, and long-distance bicyclist. Those are impressive accomplishments for any 32-year-old. However, Erik has been blind since age 13, when a degenerative eye disease destroyed his retinas.

But being blind has not prevented him from embracing all life has to offer. Recently Erik hit a new personal high by becoming the first blind climber to reach the top of Mount Everest, the tallest challenge in the world for any mountaineer.

"I just kept telling myself: 'Be focused,'" Erik explained to a CNN interviewer after his ascent. "Be full of energy. Keep relaxed. Don't let all those distractions - the fear and the doubt - creep into your brain, because that's what ruins you up there."

That's good advice for climbing any kind of mountain, be it made of rock or something more personal.

Bits & Pieces

Encountering Life's Hurdles. . . and Jumping Them

The only limit to our realization of tomorrow will be our doubts of today.

Franklin D. Roosevelt

The two high school football teams from Michigan opposed one another first on the field, and then in the courtroom. The losing team took legal action to have the victory of their opponent reversed when they found out that one of the star players from the team had played with extra equipment, an unfair advantage. The judge heard the argument, and the victory stood. His determination? The artificial leg the player in question had attached before the game was not only acceptable, it was commendable.

And speaking of football...who remembers the record setting 63 yard field goal that Tom Dempsey kicked in the game between the Detroit Lions and the New Orleans Saints in November of 1970? The kick in itself was amazing enough without knowing that Dempsey has no toes on his right foot and only half on his kicking foot.

And speaking of toes...a wonderful novel, *Down All the Days*, was published by a 37-year-old Irishman named Christy Brown. And what does this have to do with toes? Well, Mr. Brown just so happened to type the entire manuscript with the little one on his left foot. Brain damaged at birth, his vocal chords only emitted grunts, making it impossible for him to verbally dictate. He was also born without arms, unable to write out the manuscript. But what he lacked physically, he made up for in an area within his power: determination.

Hope and dreams. What are yours?

Nothing on earth can stop the man with the right mental attitude from achieving his goal, and nothing on earth can help the man with the wrong mental attitude.

Thomas Jefferson

From Crutches to a World-Class Runner

We can do only what we think we can do. We can be only what we think we can be. We can have only what we think we can have. What we do, what we are, what we have, all depend upon what we think.

Robert Collier

A number of years ago in Elkhart, Kansas, a little boy had a job at the local school. Early each morning his job was to start a fire in the potbellied stove in the classroom.

One cold morning, he cleaned out the stove and loaded it with firewood. Grabbing a can of kerosene, he doused the wood and lit the fire. An explosion then rocked the old building. It was later discovered that the kerosene can had accidentally been filled with gasoline. The fire badly burned the little boy.

The doctor attending the injured boy recommended amputating the young boy's legs. The parents were devastated, but they did not lose their faith. They asked the doctor for a postponement of the amputation, and he consented. Each day they asked the doctor for a delay, praying that their son's legs would somehow heal and that he would become well again. For two months, the parents and the doctor debated on whether to amputate. They used this time to instill in the boy the belief that he would walk again someday.

264

They never amputated the boy's legs, but when the bandages were finally removed, it was discovered that his right leg was now almost three inches shorter than the left leg. Also, the toes on the left foot were almost completely burned off. Yet the boy was fiercely determined. Though in excruciating pain, he forced himself to exercise daily and finally took a few painful steps. Slowly recovering, this young man finally threw away his crutches and began to slowly walk, then to walk almost normally. Soon he was running – and run he did.

This determined young man kept running and running and running until those legs that came so close to being amputated carried him to Madison Square Gardens where he set a record for the fastest mile ever run.

His name? Glenn Cunningham, who became known thereafter as the "World's Fastest Human Being" and was named athlete of the century.

Cunningham may have had difficulty standing up on the outside when he first began his dream, but he was standing up from within all along.

Truly, he is a champion of the heart.

Glenn Van Ekeren

To Save a Life

"Did I not tell you that if you believed, you would see..."

John 11:40

In those chaotic years of the late 1940's, just after World War II ended, an immigrant family in New York tried to contact their surviving relatives in Hungary. Communications were sporadic, the mails untrustworthy, and records destroyed or inaccurate or lost. It could take many weeks or months for letters to travel to Europe and find their way to recipients and just as long for replies to return. Reliable information was hard, if not impossible, to get.

The immigrant family wondered if their relatives were still alive. Had they all survived the war? Where were they living? It was so hard to tell. Then, they received a letter, in Hungarian, from Uncle Lazlo in a small town near Budapest. Yes, some of the family had survived the war. The letter was incomplete in the news it offered, but it was clear that they were hungry and hurting. Food and other necessities were in very short supply. The black market was operating in full force, the currency was inflated and nearly valueless. It took all their energy and wit to survive each day.

The New Yorkers were appalled at the story of devastation and deprivation they could piece together by reading and rereading the crumpled letter, written on the tissue-thin paper of the airmail of that time. Grateful to be able to read again in Hungarian, the older members of the family translated for their American-born children. They argued about the translation of this phrase or that. But it was clear that they could be useful to their far-off family.

They determined to send survival supplies to their cousins, aunts and uncles. They tried to imagine what would be needed and appreciated, but, not having directly experienced war themselves, it was not easy to come up with a list of things to send. They included canned meats, vegetables and chocolates. Necessities like toilet paper and bandages made the final list, too. In the end, the package grew to several cartons, stuffed to the brim with many items. Little spaces in each carton were filled with whatever odds and ends were at hand: candies, handkerchiefs, writing paper and pencils.

At last, the cartons were sealed and painstakingly wrapped with brown paper and string to help endure the long and chancy journey overseas. Brought to the post office, the cartons began their journey undramatically.

And that is all the New York family heard for months and months. They wondered if the packages had gone astray or been stolen. Had something terrible happened to their family in the confusion of post war Europe? What an irony it would be to have survived the war itself and be killed or injured in the aftermath. The family worried. At every dinner, at every gathering, the talk circled around the packages and the family in Europe.

The silence from their distant family was depressing,

especially in the light of the news reels they saw at the theater (television being very uncommon then) showing emaciated Europeans walking dispiritedly through rubble-strewn streets; dodging bomb craters or being deloused in long lines by GI medics. Headlines fueled their worries as newspapers wrote about the Marshall Plan and the need for much help in rebuilding war-ravaged countries. Stories circulated about people starving to death. News of a severe winter in Europe and shortages of food and fuel upset the family even more.

Although far from wealthy, the family sent more packages, off into the void, unsure as to whether or not they were received by their loved ones. More silence ensued. It was maddening.

Finally, another letter arrived from Uncle Lazlo. It had been bent, wrinkled and torn at the edges, but it was still readable.

"My Dearest Cousin," the letter began formally, as Uncle Lazlo was in the habit of writing. "We are in receipt, of three packages you sent us.

"We are forever in your debt for these good things. You cannot know how timely was their arrival. Food is so scarce here and Anna was sick all the time with fevers. This food has meant everything to us. I must confess that we sold some of the things you sent us on the black market in order to get money for our rent." The letter went on to discuss almost every item in the cartons and the uses to which they had been put. Then came a mystery.

"We also cannot thank you enough for the medicine you

sent. It is so difficult to get any medicine at all and often it is of poor potency and doesn't work. Cousin Gesher has been in continuous pain for several years and your medicine has miraculously cured him! He was walking only with the help of a cane before your medicine arrived and his knees were so swollen. But these medicines make him almost normal again. My back pain is completely gone as are Lizabeta's headaches.

"America is great and its science is great. You must send more of the medicine as it is nearly used up.

"Again, thank you. We love you all and pray for when we might see you once more."

The family read and reread Uncle Lazlo's letter. What medicine did we send? They racked their brains to recall but, shamefacedly, had to admit to each other that they had omitted sending any medicines at all! What was Uncle Lazlo talking about? Was some medicine accidentally included? If so, what was it? After all, they needed to send some more right away. The mystery couldn't be solved.

A letter was drafted to Uncle Lazlo asking him to provide the name of the medicine he so urgently required. The envelope was brought to the post office. The clerk was asked for advice on how to send the letter by the fastest route possible. There was, at the time, nothing faster than regular air mail, express services being as yet only a dream. He did suggest including an international postal reply coupon which would pay for return postage and that was done.

The family waited again, relieved that their packages had been of help but puzzled by the "mystery of the unknown medicine." Two months passed and then another letter arrived.

"My Dearest Cousins," began Uncle Lazlo, "we are grateful to have heard from you again. Since the first three packages, another two have arrived, and then your letter. Again, you sent that wonderful medicine. It did not come with instructions for use but we are guessing on the dosage. And translating from English to Hungarian is very difficult for us since only young Sandor has studied it in school. Lucky for us he could translate the name of the medicine. It is 'Life Savers'. Please send more as soon as you can. Love, Lazlo."

The filler, in several cartons, had been rolls of that well-known American candy, Life Savers. A literal translation transformed American's favorite candy into a source of great hope and belief.

Hanoch McCarty

We get what we believe we will get. Consciousness creates our lives according to its beliefs. The more limitations we impose upon our beliefs, the more we limit the creative capacity of that consciousness.

Alan Vaughan

In Sun or Storm, Evergreens Endure

If you think you can, you can. And if you think you can't, you're right.

Mary Kay

Twenty-one degrees. Not a particularly bad temperature forecast for wintertime in Wisconsin – until the radio weatherman adds those two extra little words: "below zero." Brrrrrrrrrrr.

I watch out my kitchen window as the frigid cold moves across the countryside, challenging all in its path with numbing severity. Submission is evident. Evident, but not everywhere.

Amid this surrounding harshness stand the evergreens, firm and steadfast, with a constancy strengthened from within.

Evergreens. They're everywhere. Some of them have roots and trunks and branches; others have bodies and arms and legs.

Like Wilma Rudolph. Born prematurely in 1940, the 20th of 22 children, she was not expected to survive. But she *did* survive, only to contract both scarlet fever and double pneumonia at age four. Most children would have died, but not Wilma. She lived through it, but was left paralyzed. Those are the facts.

Despite them, nine-year-old Wilma, determined not only

to walk but to run, took her leg braces off and eventually was doing both – and very well at that. By 1956 she had an Olympic bronze medal hanging around her neck, and by 1960, she had three Olympic golds. Wilma is an evergreen among us.

So is Todd Hutson. Things weren't going so well for this young man either. First, Todd was involved in a boating accident and had his legs sucked into the propeller, leaving them severely mangled. Then, infection set in. Finally, his right leg had to be amputated – not good news for someone who loved sports and the physical challenge they presented.

Well, Todd Hutson refused to surrender to his injury and, instead, rose above it – literally. This one-legged fellow started climbing mountains, accomplishing feats greater than any other he had experienced in his life before the accident. And on August 7, 1994 he accomplished his greatest of all.

On this day, Todd Hutson was standing on top of Mt. Mauna Kea in Hawaii, having just climbed 50 mountains in 66 days (including Mt. McKinley in Alaska and Mt. Hood in Oregon), having beaten the previous world record by 35 days – set by a climber in perfect health.

Todd Hutson had triumphed against all odds and is an evergreen among us.

Evergreens. They're everywhere. Some of them have roots and trunks and branches; others have bodies and arms and legs.

What Can a Quarter Buy You?

*I tell you the truth, if you have faith as small as a
mustard seed...nothing will be impossible for you.*
Matthew 17:20-21

I do believe it was the best 25 cents I had ever spent. It
went into a parking meter last Wednesday on the corner of
Sheboygan Street and Marr in Fond du Lac, Wisconsin, one
block off of the downtown area. My quarter bought me
exactly one hour of time.

Now I'd parked in this spot many times before. From
here, there is easy access to the public library. That morning,
however, instead of turning left, crossing the street, and
entering the library, I headed to the right where the
Windhover Center for the Arts is located. A friend telephoned me the day prior to let me know about a traveling
VSA (Very Special Arts) exhibit on display through the end
of the month. "You really must see this," she told me of the
collection of artwork done by disabled children.

And so here I was, beneath a bright blue sky on a very
February morn heading toward a magnificent, older building, restored to its original grandeur not long ago.

I entered and ascended several polished, wooden stairs.
Atop them, a burgundy and ivory oriental rug was laid, and
I paused on it to sign the visitor guest book.

From where I stood, the children's artwork was visible

already, hung from just beyond the double doorway entrance into the lovely gallery. The first painting - colorful, vibrant and seemingly alive - faced me. It was titled *The Dancing Flowers*. I read this and smiled, and would do so again and again during the time I spent among these children. They were not here physically, and yet they *were* here, having painted a piece of themselves onto these canvases in watercolors and oils and pastels. You could sense their presence, and you could sense who they were - and what they loved - in paintings they titled *It's Great Being Me*, *My Playroom*, *Swimming Along*, *I Enjoy It* and *The Magnificent Sunflower.*

Beside each piece a framed biography was hung listing the name, age and disability of the child. These little artists suffered from many impairments: Cerebral Palsy, Down Syndrome, Autism, Spinal Muscular Strophy, seizures, and other varied physical and emotional disabilities. Some lived in wheelchairs, like 10-year-old Brittany. There were no easy paths here. This was clear.

Yet despite challenges so enormous I could not even begin to imagine what these youngsters must face daily, each expressed himself or herself from a place of beauty within.

Like Sarah, although crippled from a disease that prevents her from even grasping onto a paintbrush, she brought forth her masterpiece, *Harvest*. How did she do this? By having a paintbrush attached to her forehead. I stop for a moment and consider Sarah, amazing Sarah, her courage leaving an impression on me that will not be forgotten - of this I am certain.

Courage is a way of life for these youngsters. And so is hope. You see it in their art, and you hear it in their words hanging beside their paintings. Eleven-year-old Julia tells us that one day she will fulfill her dream of becoming a famous woman artist. Twelve-year-old John A. Magnusson believes we can all experience the hopes our hearts harbor. He writes, "You can do anything you put your mind to." Anything. All of us. Thank you, John, for being our reminder that our dreams can take flight like the hummingbirds and butterflies and bumblebees that fill this room, painted by those "dis"abled in body, but not in soul, painted by those "focus-ing on their ability and not on their dis," as one little gal so wonderfully put it.

I left there that day a different person than the one I had been when I arrived. I knew this as I sat in a little coffee shop around the corner from the gallery sipping tea after-wards, lemon ginger with just a bit of honey, and thinking about starfish swimming in the ocean. Ten-year-old Diane Jacobson had painted several. I thought about her starfish as I stared out the large window and watched the world go by. Miss Diane believed that starfish enjoy, most of all, being together, another wonderful word.

Together, we open one another's eyes to truths we know, but have sometimes forgotten. Together, we help those unable to help themselves in some ways, and they, in turn, will help us in others. Someone, somewhere has helped these children, and I find myself profoundly grateful to each of these persons who I know not the name of, nor they mine.

We place a paintbrush in these young hands, and it is

grasped. Then something within is awakened. Or we attach such a paintbrush to a forehead and for doing so, we will be taken to places where we can see the world through beautiful, beautiful eyes, and we will be taken to places where we can look upon hope so bright where a Light shines there.

I finished my tea, and set down the sage green and orchid-colored ceramic mug I drank it from. For a while, I simply sit and admire this magnificent piece of pottery, hand-thrown and crafted by a local artist with an extraordinary talent and an ordinary name: John Smith. His work is incredibly interesting for many reasons, not the least of which is that Mr. Smith is blind.

If You Can Dream It, You Can Do It

I'm stirred when someone says, "You can't do it." I find the statement "You can't" offensive to the human spirit. We can be anything. Maybe this entire experience is a series of lessons to learn that you can – yes, you can.

Maya Angelou

Sugar Ray Robinson said, "To be a champion, you have to believe in yourself even when no one else will." Here are a few other people who would probably agree:

Marilyn Monroe was told by the director of the Blue Book Modeling Agency, "You'd better learn secretarial skills or else get married."

Buddy Holly was fired from Decca Records by Paul Cohen who called him "the biggest no talent I ever saw."

Burt Reynolds was dismissed from a Universal Studios audition in 1959 with the words, "You have no talent. None." Ironically, Clint Eastwood was in the same meeting. He was sent home, too, with the words, "You have a chip on your tooth, your Adams apple sticks out too far, and you talk too slow."

After only one performance at the Grand Ole Opry, Elvis Presley was fired by the manager who said, "You ain't goin' nowhere, son. You ought to go back to drivin' a truck."

The head instructor of the John Murray Anderson Drama School told Lucille Ball, "Try any other profession. Any

278

other."

Michael Jordan's high school basketball coach didn't think he was good enough for the team. He cut him.

Louis L'Armour, author of novels with over 200 million copies in print, received 350 rejections before he made his first sale, and Rudyard Kipling received a rejection letter from the *San Francisco Examiner* which read: "I'm sorry, Mr. Kipling, but you just don't know how to use the English language."

Fred Astaire's screen test from the director of MGM Studios reads, "Can't act. Slightly bald. Can dance *a little.*"

Walt Disney was fired by a newspaper for "lack of creativity."

Thomas Edison needed to be home schooled. His teachers gave up on him saying, "He's too stupid to learn anything."

Frank Whittle, inventor of the jet engine, showed his plans to the Professor of Aeronautical Engineering of Cambridge University who told him, "Very interesting, Whittle, my boy, but it will never work."

Faith is to believe what you do not yet see; the reward of faith is to see what you believe.

Saint Augustine

Believe It, Achieve It

To deem any situation impossible is to make it so.
Bernard Drummond

In the Star Wars movie, *The Empire Strikes Back*, Luke Skywalker flies his spaceship to a swamp planet on a personal quest. There he seeks out a Jedi master named Yoda to teach him the ways of becoming a Jedi warrior. Luke wants to free the galaxy from the oppression of the evil tyrant, Darth Vader.

Yoda agrees to help Luke and begins by teaching him how to lift rocks with his mental powers.

Then, one day, Yoda tells Luke to lift his ship out from the swamp where it sank after a crash landing. Luke complains that lifting rocks is one thing, but lifting a star-fighter spaceship is quite another matter. Yoda insists. Luke manages a valiant effort but fails in his attempt.

Yoda then focuses his mind, and lifts the ship with ease. Luke, dismayed, exclaims, "I don't believe it!"

"That's why you couldn't lift it," Yoda replied. "You didn't believe you could."

Mark Link

The Big Picture

The very least you can do in your life is to figure out what you hope for. And the most you can do is live inside that hope - not admire it from a distance, but live right in it, under its roof.

Barbara Kingsolver

Would you get into a taxi and tell the cabby, "Drive anywhere"?

Would you wander onto the first plane you saw at the airport gate without bothering to ask where it's flying to?

Of course not!!! Yet it's amazing how unfocused we can be about the biggest asset we have - our lives.

Goals shouldn't be blurry, half-baked, or fuzzy. Living a deliberate life requires being focused because today you're living out the choices you are making today.

The more precise, exact, streamlined, and specific you are about where you're going, the more powerful your life will be. It's like painting by numbers in reverse.

First comes the big picture, then the bits that make the big picture complete.

Deborah Rosado Shaw

How Old is Too Old?

A positive attitude is a magnet for positive results.
Anonymous

Did you know that the world-famous pianist Artur Rubinstein gave one of his greatest recitals at age 89?

Or that Tintoretto, the great 16th century Renaissance artist, painted "Paradise" when he was 74? (It was a canvas measuring 74 feet by 30 feet!!)

Did you know that another great Renaissance artist, Titian, painted his historic picture of the "Battle of Lepanto" when he was 98?

Or that the celebrated American artist, Grandma Moses, didn't even begin painting until she was 78 - *and never even had an art lesson*?

Then there's the German writer, Goethe, who completed his masterpiece "Faust," when he was 80; and Tennyson, the 19th century English writer, who made profound contributions to world literature throughout his lifetime, including "Crossing the Bar" - written when he was 83.

There's Oliver Wendell Holmes, the American poet, novelist, and physician, who wrote "Over the Teacups" at 79; and Verdi who gave the world his famous "Ave Maria" when he was 85.

And there's architect Frank Lloyd Wright who was asked at age 83 which of his works he would select as his masterpiece. He replied, "My next one."

Their accomplishments leave the question "How old is too old?" unanswered.

Only you can deprive yourself of anything. Do not oppose this realization, for it is truly the beginning of the dawn of light.

A Course in Miracles

Chapter 5 – Summary

If You Believe, You Will See

There is a law in psychology that if you form a picture in your mind of what you would like to be, and you keep and hold that picture there long enough, you will soon become exactly as you have been thinking.

William James

What are your hopes? What are your dreams? Do you believe that you can reach them?

Step number one in reaching a goal is determining what your goal is. Step number two is maintaining a positive expectation of meeting it. Each of these steps is rooted in the same divine formula that can be used to draw more love, peace and joy into our lives.

The simplest explanation as to how the formula can be used to fulfill goals is this: When positive expectation is released regarding the outcome of a situation, this positive energy pulls other positive energy into our life, helping us along our way. The same is true of doubt. When doubt and fear are released, they, too, connect with energy, but it is a negative energy that is pulled in, an energy that will work directly against us. Thus, a person's own doubt becomes his or her greatest obstacle, blocking access to positive energy and positive results; a person's own fear becomes the most significant hindrance to experiencing the best life has to offer each of us. Doubt creates more doubt. Fear does the same.

In the preceding stories, examples were given to illustrate "really happened" successes that began with hope. Seemingly impossible dreams started coming true for persons up against staggering odds: a blind man who wanted to ski, an amputee who wanted to climb mountains, and for a young man who was told he would never walk again but set his heart on becoming a world-class runner. How did these incredible, incredible dreams come true? Simple: their possessors didn't expect them not to.

Although these real stories about real people detail different accomplishments, there is one common denominator within each. It is this: each person held fast to an unshakable confidence and an unwaveringly hope in reaching their desired destinations – and hope is a powerful thing. It, too, multiplies upon itself, creating more hope, and more and more.

"We begin to receive when we begin to believe." This single sentence, handed down through the ages, conveys a profound spiritual truth: our beliefs release a spiritual power in our lives. We call forth into physical existence that which first exists within our minds. This is both the good news and the bad, because faith operates, as we have discussed, in two dimensions: positive and negative - positive faith being evidenced by hope, and negative faith being evidenced by fear.

Which of these is the driving force of your life: positive or negative energy? Do you generally believe more often than not that things will turn out for the best or do you expect them to turn out for the worst? Spend some time today thinking about your answers to these questions and reminding yourself that what you believe, you will receive. These simple reflections can significantly raise your awareness as to how much of your thinking is rooted in doubt.

Several years ago, I completed a Bible study on the subject of fear. It was fascinating to me to discover that there are 365 specific warnings about the power of negative faith found in the attitudes of fear and doubt. Scripture after scripture, included warnings to "fear not, worry not, be not afraid, be not terrified, have faith and do not doubt." A reminder was provided for every single day of the year. I wondered why.

I believe the answer to that very question is found in the Biblical book of James 1:6-8 where we are told we "must believe and not doubt because he who doubts is like a wave of the sea, blown and tossed by the wind. That man should not think he will receive anything...he is a double-minded man, unstable in all he does."

In all honesty, these verses bothered me for a good long time. I simply could not understand why Heaven would withhold goodness from a person simply because he or she was fearful or doubtful. But then it clicked: Heaven doesn't withhold anything from us. *We* withhold.

When we are hoping for something positive, we are sending out a positive energy. This energy has the power to create what we believe. But then, if we begin to doubt what we hope for, we are sending out a negative energy which will negate the original positive force. We receive "nothing" because the energy is returned to zero. A positive combined with a negative will mathematically yield an end result of zero.

The analogy of a wave, blown and tossed, is quite fitting. How often do we find ourselves believing something good will happen, but then end up convincing ourselves it probably won't? "Yes it will, no it won't; yes it will, no it won't." We toss back and forth in double mindedness and accomplish little or nothing. Fear. Its grip is powerful, leaving us helpless and defeated when we submit to it.

How does one begin the process of replacing fear with faith? How does positive faith operate?

Positive faith is released – as the Scriptures reveal - "through love." And so, as we stand in positive faith in regards to our hopes and dreams, we must also stand in positive faith in our commitment to love others. Our life is one big picture. Everything is connected. Everything matters.

At first glance, a chapter on achieving one's dreams would seem out of place with the preceding chapters dealing with kindness, generosity, forgiveness and anger. However, the connection between living a loving life and living an accomplished life is undeniable.

As an example, we find in Mark's Gospel one of many direct links between powerful living and our relationships with others. In chapter 11, verses 22-25 we read: "Have faith in God...I tell you the truth, if anyone says to this mountain, 'Go, throw yourself into the sea,' and does not doubt in his heart but believes that what he says will happen, it will be done for him. Therefore I tell you, whatever you ask for in prayer, believe that you have received it, and it will be yours. And when you stand praying, if you hold anything against anyone, forgive."

Two seemingly unrelated subjects are lined up side-by-side in this teaching: belief and forgiveness. The message of these words is clear: Fear will block our paths – every aspect of fear, including unforgiveness. The negative attitudes of fear manifested in any form - resentment, anger, doubt or hate - are spiritual roadblocks that work directly against the power of positive faith which operates through love. Our attitudes toward life, and our attitudes toward others, are directly linked to our goals.

Goals. What are yours? Are you ready to begin to believe and achieve?

If so, first determine what your goals are. Get clear on what it is you want. Narrow it down. What is it *exactly*?

After you begin to focus on what your goals are, get a mental picture of them within your mind. Visualize your expectations. "See" yourself succeeding. When a positive image is sent forth from your mind, an important step is taken toward the materialization of your vision into reality.

Next, remind yourself: "If I don't believe, I won't receive." Understanding this concept is key. It is absolutely, positively key. As important as it is to get decisive about what your goals are, it is equally important to believe that you can reach them.

If self-doubt persists, re-read the true stories given as examples in this chapter in order to reinforce your understanding of the fact that nothing is impossible. Consider each story and reflect on the extreme challenges that were overcome by sheer human determination stretched to remarkable limits, stories about individuals who easily could have allowed the circumstances of their lives to convince them that all was hopeless. But instead, they decided that their lives would not be defined by their circumstances. They determined that they would be bigger than their circumstances and bigger than their obstacles. Each remained open to believing that Life still offered infinite possibilities. Rather than focusing on the "why" question of their handicap or their past, they focused on the "where" they intended to go from that point on and "how" they intended to get there. "Where," "how," and "when" are positive questions we can ask ourselves, questions that will call us to action and responsibility.

Know this: it matters not nearly as much where you have been, as it does where you are committed to go from here. Regardless if your life before this moment has been filled with regrets, what matters most is not what you have done in the past, or where you have been, but what you now intend to do with where you have been and with what you have done.

Right now, at this moment, your life can begin changing for the better - and for the best. Each of us has equal access to positive mental mindsets and loving attitudes that are the driving force behind successful living. When we commit to livingly lovingly, and when we commit to replacing our self-doubts, our self-condemnations, our fears and our excuses -

"I'm too young, too old, too poor, too inexperienced" - with positive actions and positive beliefs, great things happen.

Through consistent, small steps made daily, we begin to discover these small steps are yielding big differences in our lives. Every effort we put forth toward achieving our goals multiplies unto itself until we find ourselves living our best life, a life that has evolved from our dream into our reality.

Permissions

"Harvesting a Bumper Crop of Blessings" by Rochelle Pennington.

"The Multiplication Table of God" by Rochelle Pennington.

"We Cannot Give Without Receiving" by William Arthur Ward. Used by permission of Mrs. Margaret V. Ward.

"What are the Odds?" by Frank Christian. © 1998. Used by permission of author.

"Life's Mirror" by Madeline Bridges. Public Domain.

"Things Turned Rosy" by Yitta Halberstam and Judith Leventhal from *Small Miracles.* © 1997. Used by permission of Adams Media Corporation.

"To Give or Not to Give" by Harry Emerson Fosdick. Public Domain.

"A Change of Heart" by Rochelle Pennington.

"Choosing the Way of Your Soul" by William Dunkerley, pen name John Oxenham. Public Domain.

"Arthur Berry's Answer" by Dale Galloway from *How to Feel Like a Somebody Again,* © 1986. Used by permission of author.

"Echo, Echo, Echo" by Arthur Gordon, © 2000. Used by permission of Mrs. Pamela Gordon per Authur Gordon's Estate.

"Even in the Little Things" from *God's Little Daily Devotional.* © 1997. Used by permission of Honor Books, Tulsa, OK.

"God's Circle" by H. S. Smith. © 1888. Public Domain.

Quotation by Chuck Vrtacek from *Coincidences. Touched by a Miracle* by Antoinette Bosco, © 1998. Used by permission of Twenty-Third Publications, Mystic, CT.

"One Good Turn Deserves Another" from *Incredible Coincidence: The Baffling World of Synchronicity* by Alan Vaughan. © 1979 by Alan Vaughan. Reprinted by permission of HarperCollins Publishers, Inc.

"Elijah – God's Prophet" from NIV Bible.

Permissions

"Have Faith" by Bruce Larson from *The Edge of Adventure*, © 1974, Word Books, Waco, TX. Used by permission of author.

"Mercury and the Woodman" by Aesop. Public Domain.

"The Beggar King" excerpted from *More Sower's Seeds* by Brian Cavanaugh. © 1992. Used by permission of Paulist Press. Available at bookstores or www.paulistpress.com or 1-800-218-1903.

"From a Kernel to Abundance" by Glenn Van Ekeren from THE SPEAKER'S SOURCEBOOK. © 1988. Reprinted with permission of Prentice Hall Direct.

"What I've Learned So Far" from *Complete Live and Learn and Pass It On* by H. Jackson Brown, Jr., © 1998 and reprinted by permission of Rutledge Hill Press, Nashville, Tennessee.

"Delayed But Not Denied" by Reverend Robb Thompson. Used by permission of author, © 2001 by Family Harvest Church.

"A Chance Encounter" from *God's Little Daily Devotional*. © 1997. Used by permission of Honor Books, Tulsa, OK.

"A Mysterious Benefactor" by Paul Aurandt. Excerpt from pp. 37-8 from DESTINY by Paul Aurandt, © 1983 by Paulynne, Inc. Reprinted by permission of HarperCollins Publishers, Inc.

"A Circle of Happiness" excerpted from *The Practice of Kindness* by the Editors of Conari Press, © 1996 by Conari Press, used by permission of Conari Press.

"Heart Gifts" by Pam Smith. Used by permission of author, © 2002.

"Living Our Best Lives" by Rochelle Pennington.

"Love is the Lifter of the Human Soul" by Rochelle Pennington. Pennington's retold public domain story is adapted from "It's in Your Hands, Son" as retold by Glenn Van Ekeren in THE SPEAKER'S SOURCEBOOK. © 1988. Reprinted with permission of Prentice Hall Direct.

"Ripples" by Cheryl Kirking. Used by permission of author. © 1998 Cheryl Kirking/Mill Pond Music from the CD "100 Ripples" and included in the book *Ripples of Joy*.

"Appointment With Destiny" by Yitta Halberstam and Judith Leventhal from *Small Miracles II*. © 1998. Used by permission of Adams Media Corporation.

Permissions

"It Will Be Given to You" by Mark Link from *Action*, © 1994 Mark Link, S. J. Reprinted by permission of Thomas More Publishing, Allen, Texas 75002.

"Giving and Receiving" by Billie Davis, quoted from *The Pentecostal Evangel*, March 17, 1996. © 1996 Billie Davis. Used by permission of author.

"Pass It On" by Anne Brandt. Used by permission of author, © 2002.

"The Farnham Legacy" by Bert F. Engstrom, DMD. Used by permission of author, © 2001.

"Androcles Revisited" by Paul Aurandt. Excerpt from pp.67-70 from MORE OF PAUL HARVEY'S THE REST OF THE STORY by PAUL AURANDT. © 1980 by PAULYNNE, INC. Reprinted by permission of HarperCollins Publishers, Inc.

"How Could I Miss, I'm a Teacher!" by Hanoch McCarty. © 1997, 2002, Hanoch McCarty, Ed.D. All rights reserved. Originally published in *A 4th Course of Chicken Soup for the Soul* by Jack Canfield, Mark Victor Hansen, Hanoch McCarty and Meladee McCarty, 1997.

"The Man Who Missed Christmas" by J. Edgar Park. Reprinted with permission from *Guideposts* magazine. © 1955 by Guideposts, Carmel, New York 10512.

"The Sin of Omission" by Margaret E. Sangster. Public Domain.

"A Giving Tree" excerpted from *Sower's Seeds of Encouragement* by Brian Cavanaugh. © 1998. Used by permission of Paulist Press. Available at bookstores or www.paulist-press.com or 1-800-218-1903.

"Silas Peterman's Investment" by Susan Huffner Martin. Published in *Heart to Heart Stories of Friendship*, Tyndale House Publishers, Inc., 1999. Text used by permission of Review and Herald Publishing Association, Hagerstown, MD 21740, and Joe L. Wheeler, P.O. Box 1246, Conifer, CO 80433.

Quotation excerpted from *The Practice of Kindness* by the Editors of Conari Press, © 1996 by Conari Press, used by permission of Conari Press.

"What Constitutes Quality Human Relationships?" by Glenn Van Ekeren from THE SPEAKER'S SOURCEBOOK. © 1988. Reprinted with permission of Prentice Hall Direct. Original story title: "Do Unto Others."

"Perfect Timing" by Roman Turski excerpted from the article "Turn About". Reprinted with permission from the January 1953 Reader's Digest. © 1953 by The Reader's Digest

295

Permissions

Assn., Inc.

"We Will Meet Again" by Author Unknown.

"The Golden Rule Revisited" by Dr. Edwin Leap from *Emergency Medical News*, October 2000, page 18. Used by permission of Lippincott Williams & Wilkins, New York, New York, © 2000.

"Together We Can Make It" by Dan Clark from *Puppies For Sale*, © 2000. Used by permission of author.

"Love is the Crowning Glory" by Rochelle Pennington.

"Charitable Giving, Charitable Living" by Rochelle Pennington.

"Raising the Bar" by Rochelle Pennington.

"The Bible" by Beckah Fink as seen in DEAR ABBY by Abigail Van Buren a.k.a. Jeanne Phillips and founded by her mother Pauline Phillips. © Universal Press Syndicate. Reprinted with permission. All rights reserved.

"Life is an Empty Bottle" excerpted from *Sower's Seeds Aplenty* by Brian Cavanaugh. © 1996. Used by permission of Paulist Press. Available at bookstores or www.paulist-press.com or 1-800-218-1903.

"The Law of Life" by Jerry Buchanan. © 1991. Used by permission of Ms. Jean Buchanan.

"Loving Your Enemies" excerpted from *Sower's Seeds of Virtue* by Brian Cavanaugh. © 1997. Used by permission of Paulist Press. Available at bookstores or www.paulist-press.com or 1-800-218-1903.

"Unto Thee I Grant: The Understanding of Anger" by Tibetan Wisdom. Public Domain.

"Goodwill, Ill Will" by Norman Vincent Peale. Used by permission of the Peale Foundation, Pawling, New York.

"Anger's Poisonous Bite" by Mark Link from *Action*, © 1994 Mark Link, S. J. Reprinted by permission of Thomas More Publishing, Allen, Texas 75002.

"Love Your Enemy" by Corrie ten Boom. Excerpted from "I'm Still Learning to Forgive" by Corrie ten Boom. Reprinted with permission from *Guideposts* magazine. © 1972 by Guideposts, Carmel, New York 10512.

Permissions

"Love is Vital" by Jo Ann Larsen from *The Heart of Goodness,* © 1999. Used by permission of Shadow Mountain, Salt Lake City, Utah.

"What is the Meaning of Life?" by Robert Fulghum from IT WAS ON FIRE WHEN I LAY DOWN ON IT by Robert Fulghum, © 1988, 1989 by Robert Fulghum. Used by permission of Villard Books, a division of Random House, Inc.

"Prayer of Peace" by St. Francis of Assisi. Public Domain.

"Carl's Garden" by Author Unknown.

"Forgiving an Enemy" from *God's Little Daily Devotional.* © 1997. Used by permission of Honor Books, Tulsa, OK.

"What is the Perfect Gift?" by Rochelle Pennington.

"The House by the Side of the Road" by Sam Walter Foss. Public Domain.

"A Word of Warning" by Rochelle Pennington.

"Defining Heaven and Hell" by Jack Kornfield and Christina Feldman from *Stories of the Spirit, Stories of the Heart,* © 1991. Used by permission of author.

"Paco Come Home" by Alan Cohen. Used by permission of author. Alan Cohen is the author of the bestselling book *The Dragon Doesn't Live Here Anymore.* To order your copy of Alan's new book, *Why Your Life Sucks and What You Can Do About It,* visit your local bookstore or log on to www.amazon.com. For a free catalog of Alan's books, tapes, and seminars, or to receive his free newsletter, email admin@alancohen.com, phone 1-800-568-3079, or write P.O. Box 835, Haiku, HI 96708. Visit Alan's web site at www.spiritfirst.com.

"Forgive, Forgive, Forgive" by Rochelle Pennington.

"The Most Powerful Word in the World" by Rochelle Pennington.

"A Lesson in Gratitude" from *The Best of Bits & Pieces* © 1994. Used by permission of Ragan Communication, Chicago, IL.

"Thank You, God" by Margaret Jarek. Used by permission of author, © 2002.

"The Power of Gratitude" by Sarah Ban Breathnach from THE SIMPLE ABUNDANCE JOURNAL OF GRATITUDE. © 1996 by Sarah Ban Breathnach. Used by permission of Warner Books, Inc.

Permissions

"Learning Gratitude" by Alan Loy McGinnis from THE POWER OF OPTIMISM. © 1990 by Alan Loy McGinnis. Reprinted by permission of HarperCollins Publishers Inc.

"Four Magic Words" by Glenn Van Ekeren from THE SPEAKER'S SOURCEBOOK. © 1988. Reprinted with permission of Prentice Hall Direct. Original story title: "I Thank Thee, Lord."

"The Richness of Life's Simple Pleasures" by Rochelle Pennington.

"The Driving Force of My Survival" by Robert J. Morgan excerpted from MORE

REAL STORIES FOR THE SOUL. © 2000. Used by permission of Thomas Nelson Publishers, Nashville, Tennessee.

"Surrender to Negative or Strive for Positive" by Margaret Jarek. Used by permission of author, © 2002.

"How We Look at Things" excerpted from *The Sower's Seeds* by Brian Cavanaugh. © 1990. Used by permission of Paulist Press. Available at bookstores or www.paulist-press.com or 1-800-218-1903.

"A Philosophy for Life" by Mahatma Gandhi. Public Domain.

"As You Think" by James Allen. Edited version by Marc Allen © 1998 used by permission of New World Library, Novato, CA. Original version by James Allen from *As a Man Thinketh*, © 1904. Public Domain.

"Choosing Your Mindset" by Alan Loy McGinnis from THE POWER OF OPTIMISM. © 1990 by Alan Loy McGinnis. Reprinted by permission of HarperCollins Publishers Inc.

"Granny's Glasses" by Walter Buchanan from *Pulpit Helps*, Volume 14, #2. Used by permission of AMG Publishers, Chattanooga, TN.

"What Do You See?" As retold by Rochelle Pennington.

"Be Happy Where You Are" by Alan Loy McGinnis from THE POWER OF OPTIMISM. © 1990 by Alan Loy McGinnis. Reprinted by permission of HarperCollins Publishers Inc.

"All These Things" by Robert J. Morgan excerpted from MORE REAL STORIES FOR THE SOUL. © 2000. Used by permission of Thomas Nelson Publishers, Nashville, Tennessee.

Permissions

"The Wooden Sword" retold by Heather Forest, excerpted from WISDOM TALES FROM AROUND THE WORLD. © 1996 by Heather Forest. Used by permission of August House Publishers, Inc., P.O. Box 3223, Little Rock, Arkansas 72203.

"Unleashing Gratitude's Power" by Rochelle Pennington.

"Aspire Higher" by Rochelle Pennington.

"Surmounting Life's Peaks" from *Bits & Pieces,* 08/09/2001 issue, page 12 © 2001. Used by permission of Ragan Communication, Chicago, IL.

"Encountering Life's Hurdles...and Jumping Them" by Rochelle Pennington.

"From Crutches to a World-Class Runner" by Glenn Van Ekeren from THE SPEAK-ER'S SOURCEBOOK. © 1988. Reprinted with permission of Prentice Hall Direct.

"To Save a Life" by Hanoch McCarty.© 1997, 2002, Hanoch McCarty, Ed.D. All rights reserved. Originally published in *A 4th Course of Chicken Soup for the Soul* by Jack Canfield, Mark Victor Hansen, Hanoch McCarty and Meladee McCarty, 1997.

"In Sun or Storm, Evergreens Endure" by Rochelle Pennington.

"What Can a Quarter Buy You?" by Rochelle Pennington.

"If You Can Dream It, You Can Do It" by Rochelle Pennington.

"Believe It, Achieve It" by Mark Link from *Challenge,* © 1993 Mark Link, S. J. Reprinted by permission of Thomas More Publishing, Allen, Texas 75002.

"The Big Picture" by Deborah Rosado Shaw. Reprinted with the permission of The Free Press, an imprint of Simon & Schuster Adult Publishing Group, from DREAM BIG! A Roadmap for Facing Life's Challenges and Creating the Life You Deserve by Deborah Rosado Shaw. © 2001 by Dream Big! Enterprises, LLC.

"How Old is Too Old?" by Rochelle Pennington.

"If You Believe, You Will See" by Rochelle Pennington.

The Golden Formula, Volume II

If you have a story that is especially meaningful and would like for us to share it with readers in the next edition of *The Golden Formula*, please write and tell us about it.

We welcome original stories you have written and also stories you found in a newspaper, newsletter, magazine, or even in another book.

We look forward to hearing from you!

The Golden Formula
c/o Rochelle M. Pennington
P.O. Box 331
Campbellsport, WI 53010

For each story, please give the author's name along with the original source of the story if it was previously published.

We may not be able to personally contact everyone who submits a story, but we will notify you if the story you submitted is used.

With gratitude,
Pathways Press

Cover illustrator, Renee Sleger, from Houston, Texas, has earned distinguished recognition during her past twenty-five years as a portrait and mural artist.

Best known for her custom portraits of children, she can be reached directly at: 1-979-992-3982.

The Golden Formula is available through
your local bookstore or by calling:
1-800-503-5507